THE PLEASURE BOOK

THE PLEASURE BOOK

JULIUS FAST

STEIN AND DAY/*Publishers*/New York

First published in 1975
Copyright © 1975 by Julius Fast
All rights reserved
Designed by David Miller
Printed in the United States of America
Stein and Day/*Publishers*/Scarborough House,
Briarcliff Manor, N.Y. 10510

SECOND PRINTING, 1975

Library of Congress Cataloging in Publication Data

Fast, Julius, 1918–
 The pleasure book.

 1. Pleasure. I. Title.
BS515.F23   152.4′4   75-15815
ISBN 0-8128-1871-7

For Tim, Melissa, Jennifer,
Dan, Barbara, and all the others .

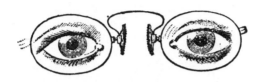

Contents

THE PLEASURE BOOK

Introduction:

The Principles of Pleasure

In a little antiques store in the country I found a framed, cross-stitched motto from the 1800's. Instead of the usual *God bless our happy home*, it read *Idle hands find pleasure in needlework*.

It was so charming that I bought it and showed it to my friend Florence, a lady quick with the needles. "Is there really any pleasure in needlework?" I asked her.

"It's a real turn-on," she said, and went on to tell me about the enjoyment she got from it.

Discarding my macho hang-ups, I decided to take a stab at needlework myself. To my surprise, I loved it. Then I wondered: How many pleasures do we all miss just because we're not aware of them or afraid to try them?

I made it my goal to uncover things other people enjoyed, things I had never thought of as pleasure, and open my mind to them. For instance, golf was an absolute mystery to me. I never understood why a grown man would want to hit a little ball around the green.

But then I spoke to John, and I became intrigued with the game. Since then I've had some wonderful days on the fairway.

Another discovery was ballooning. I thought it had gone out of style in the nineteenth century, but to my amazement I found it a thriving sport in America today.

Sailplaning, fireworks, massage, weeds—the list grew. Some of my best friends got enjoyment out of things I had never thought of doing—and some of them had crazy, secret pleasures. They all had friends who had friends who had friends . . . I found that people loved to talk about their pleasures, and listening to them was a pleasure in itself.

Pleasure is, of course, extremely subjective. What turns one person on can turn another off, but as we discover new pleasures, we expand our ability to experience new feelings—emotionally, intellectually, physically.

PURSUIT OF PLEASURE

Most of us have a favorite pleasure—one act, one situation above all others that we enjoy more than all the rest. Too often, unfortunately, we're locked into just that one thing, and forget that there are so many other possible pleasures in life. John, the golfer, may get nothing but sore fingers out of needlework, while Florence feels no urge to get out on a fairway.

There is no reason, however, why each person can't pursue more than one pleasure. A broad spectrum of possible fun is available to all of us. Why should anyone zero in on just one band of the spectrum?

This book will explore some of the vast number of available pleasures in order to show how you can use a variety of activities and states of awareness to increase your own enjoyment. It will show you how to turn on to the pleasures of other people, to educate yourself to respond to a multitude of stimuli.

The key to responding to new pleasures is the ability to focus your consciousness on new things and new ways of perceiving old, familiar things. There's a trick to turning the corner of perception and looking back from a slightly different angle.

A walk in the rain, for example, may be an uncomfortable experience for many of us. Our clothes grow damp, our bodies chill, and our feet wet. But from a different viewpoint, a walk in the rain can be pleasure. There is a visual joy to be found in houses, trees, and flowers in a shower. Rain brings out different scents; there is a tactile pleasure when raindrops fall on our skin, as well as a poetic pleasure in seeing a rain-swept city street or country road.

Part of the secret of enjoying new experiences is to achieve an altered state of consciousness, where we can let our senses rise above the minor discomfort of cold and damp to respond to the swelling tide of sensual stimulation.

Unfortunately, many of us tend to feel that too much pleasure is in some way harmful. Perhaps it pulls us away from reality. We feel that the man or woman too involved in pleasure is unable to cope with life.

Guilt also works to thin out our pleasure. How many of us, after a good meal, have ordered a particularly luscious dessert and then felt too guilty to eat it? Who has not gone on a vacation and then felt too guilty to enjoy it?

STRENGTHENING OUR INNER SELVES

Part of learning how to derive more pleasure out of life consists in overcoming that kind of reservation. The other part lies in doing away with our conviction that if pleasure comes easily, it must be bad. The old Puritan ethic tells us we must work hard for every good experience we get. If one comes without hard work, we feel guilty, and the guilt works to inhibit our joy in the experience. We are caught in a vicious circle.

But in reality, undeserved pleasure can do us a world of good. Pleasure-giving experiences are always linked to our expectations, our health, and our awareness. If we expect to enjoy an experience, we probably will. If we're convinced we won't like it, no pleasure can possibly result.

The same is true of our body condition. If we are healthy and in good physical shape, we respond to pleasure more easily. If we are aware of our bodies and all our senses, our responses are heightened.

Ultimately, an increased ability to feel pleasure will make our inner selves stronger. There is an unconscious reasoning that if we allow ourselves to have pleasure, it means that we are worth that pleasure, that we have more value as a person. If you have this outlook, you automatically think more of yourself. You have higher self-esteem, a better outlook on life, and a greater ability to enjoy.

THE RESOURCES OF PLEASURE

Scientists at the University of Kansas who studied the human response to pleasure in great detail discovered that we experience pleasure "in proportion to the frequency of our resources." In other words, the more sources of pleasure we have, the happier we are.

The scientists break these "resources, " or sources of pleasure, into three groups:

Informational resources—those that give us knowledge about other resources.

Environmental resources—the ones that exist outside ourselves, whether other people or physical objects.

Personal resources—those within ourselves.

This book is designed to turn you on to other people's resources. You'll discover why they get a kick out of doing things as different as sitting in the dark and checking into lavish hotels.

After talking to hundreds of people, I selected the most articulate to tell you about the things they enjoy the most. Perhaps, after reading these brief interviews, you'll decide to try some of the pleasures they describe and increase your own potential for happiness. I've avoided putting the pleasures in any logical order, but there is an alphabetical index to help you find your favorites.

This is a book for browsing. Pick it up and open it at random.

Then think about whatever pleasures you come across. Mull them over and try to picture yourself white-watering down a creek in an inner tube, building a sand castle, baking bread, or experimenting with one of the other ideas in this hedonist's guide. You just might find yourself trying a few—and enjoying them.

My Father's Castles

"One of my pleasantest childhood memories," Herb tells me, "is of my father building a sand castle for me and my brothers and sister. There was always a lot of preparation involved. He'd have to hunt for just the right kind of shells and driftwood for digging—he'd never let us use our tin pails or shovels.

"He had a very definite technique, my father. He'd build his sand castle from the top down."

"How could he do that?"

"Well, first he'd find the spot where the sand was just damp enough to hold together, and that was a number all in itself. He'd test each spot very solemnly by making a small sample square out of sand, and then stressing it to see if it would hold properly —while we kids watched breathlessly. I don't know how much of it was for real and how much was for our benefit.

"When he finally found just the right spot, just the proper distance from the water—first you had to determine whether the tide was coming in or going out—with just the right consistency of sand, then he'd mark out an area and all of us kids would get to work. Basically, we were the slave labor that built the castle. We'd dig a moat along the line he had indicated, and with the sand we dug out we'd make a great big mound, as high as the castle was to be.

"When the moat was dug, if the mound still wasn't high enough, we'd find another spot with the same kind of sand and carry it over to our castle. That was the real hard work, and we kids had to do it while my father supervised. The mound had to be packed just right, and by the time we were finished we'd be thoroughly exhausted and ready to sit back and watch while my father, the expert, took over.

"He always approached it carefully, studying the mound of sand from all the different angles. 'A castle can't just be built,' he'd tell us when our impatience got the better of us. 'It has to face a certain way. We have to consider invasion from the sea as well as the land.'

"When he had all his angles surveyed, all his approaches determined, he'd start to work. He would begin from the top, cutting the skyline of the castle, the crenellated ramparts and battlements, the cone-shaped towers, the long walls between. Then he would begin to cut down, shaping the walls and under-cutting the edges of the ramparts. That undercutting was the most delicate part of all, and we'd sit there holding our breath. It was so easy for a section of the wall to crumble if the undercutting was too deep, or if the dampness of the sand had been underestimated.

"Then, finally, the castle would be almost done, the walls carved down to the ground, and the final, delicate job of cutting archways and doors would be completed. Then there was a period of admiring, when we'd all gather around, viewing it from every angle, speculating on how well it could be defended, how strategically it could be taken, how exciting its battlements looked against the sky, especially if you lay on your stomach to view it.

"Then someone would run to get our mother, and she would come down and give it the final inspection while we all watched. Finally she would nod and say, 'I do think it's one of your better efforts, Henry.'

"Then it would be our turn again. 'The important thing,' our father would tell us, 'is to protect it against its real enemy, the sea,' and we'd all stare anxiously at the waterline. Was the tide ready to come in? We knew what we had to do to protect it, and we'd all pitch in, digging long channels between the castle and the ocean to drain away the incoming tide, wall after wall for the tides to broach before they could lap at the castle doors, and there was always one of us, carried away, who insisted on extra fortifications on the land side—you never knew who could attack from the dunes.

"My father would wander off with my mother then and we kids would take over the castle to play with until the tides came, or one of the walls dried out enough to collapse. We'd people it with soldiers made out of shells and seaweed and sticks, and we'd tear flags and pennants out of paper and fly them from the towers. It was such great fun."

"Have you ever done it with your children?"

Herb nods. "It's not quite the same. My own kids don't seem to have the patience we had. They lose interest and tell me, 'It's only a sand castle, Dad. Don't fuss so much.' And then too, I had to build it differently. I start with the kids' tin pails and pack them with sand, then use them as molds for the towers and build the crenellated walls between. But my castles are all smaller than my father's, less complicated—or maybe I just remember them as bigger. The whole world was bigger then.

"But I still get a tremendous amount of pleasure out of building the castles—even when my kids wander off and I have to finish them myself. I guess the pleasure is nostalgic. Sand castles take me back to the pleasantest time of my childhood.

"It's funny, last summer I saw another father building his kid a castle by dripping very wet sand in piles. As the sand dried, each pile would look like a stalagmite. I stopped to talk to him and discovered that he too was trying to duplicate the castles his father had built. 'As I remember them,' he told me, looking ruefully at his small piles, 'my father's castles soared. They reminded me of Gaudí's Art Nouveau buildings in Spain. They weren't piles of sand. They were spires and delicate fairy towers, a little mad or wild, but they were castles! These'—he shrugged and dribbled another handful of wet sand—'they're not the same.'

"I knew better than to comfort him, and I walked away, wondering what kind of castles my father's father had built."

The Pleasures of the Night

Barbara, a high school teacher, says being alone at night can fill her with pleasure.

"I discovered it when I was in my early teens. I read a poem with a line that spoke of the joy you feel 'If ever you've dropped white, white stones into a moonlit pool.'

"I puzzled over that poem for most of a winter, and that summer, working as a waitress at a hotel resort, I found a quiet forest pool out behind the cabin where we slept. I collected a handful of very white stones, and stayed up till after two one brilliant, moonlit night—or morning.

"I had marked the path to the pool during the day, but the moon was so bright I had no trouble finding my way. I squatted in the ferns at the water's edge, and one by one I dropped my stones into the water. I don't know what I expected, maybe some hidden revelation or understanding, or even a sense of joy, but there was nothing but the splash of the pebbles and a widening circle of ripples."

She laughed. "I was only a kid, and I was disappointed, ready to go back to my cabin and comfortable bed. But as long as I'd taken all this trouble I was reluctant to leave. Weren't my stones white enough? Had I missed some essential point about the verse?

"Sitting there by the moonlit water, I became aware of the night sounds, the insect noises, and now and then the cry of a bird. I watched the water and the shape of the trees beyond it. On the far bank I saw a line of reeds, silver-white in the moonlight.

"I looked up at the moon and watched a ragged edge of cloud pass across it. There was a momentary illusion that the moon itself was rushing through the sky. Now I noticed the sky for the first time, not quite black, but not blue—just a velvet combination of both.

"The silence around me became more intense because of the night noises, the way a picture is enhanced by a frame. A white moth fluttered past, its wings glowing against the darkness, and near the water's edge I heard a soft rustle in the grass—an animal come to drink!"

Barbara smiled, her eyes far away in time. "Not all at once, but gradually, as I sat there, a deep sense of pleasure filled me. I had a sense of bodily well-being, as if some quality in the night, some part of the dark, was flowing into me. I leaned back and opened myself to it, letting it fill me with an absolute content.

"You know, I sat there for over two hours, unaware of time or the hard, damp ground, of any physical discomfort, too overwhelmed by the strange joy I felt to even want to think clearly."

"Was it only that night," I asked, "or did you ever feel the pleasure again?"

"Well, I never had a chance to go back to that spot, but I was able to recapture that same sense of pleasure in other places at different times. I even found it one night on the roof of a high-rise apartment house in a large city. There was only a sliver of moon, but the lights of the city softened the darkness of the sky, and the sounds of traffic filtered up sort of muted and indistinct. I sensed the silence around me, behind the noise, but an intrinsic part of the night."

She went on to tell me how she had found the same pleasure on other nights in lonely places, often unfamiliar spots, but always with the same stillness and darkness, the same sense of being one with the earth and plants and air.

I listened to Barbara, and later I tried to capture the pleasure of the night she described so well. It worked for me. I've found it in strange cities, in the desert, at the seashore, on mountain trails and the decks of ships at sea.

It seems as if the place can be almost anywhere in the world, but the conditions must be right, with a hint of a moon to soften the darkness so that you can distinguish forms, but not detail. There has to be a stillness beyond the night noises, and you must bring to the moment your own receptiveness.

Try it. You'll be surprised how often you can find the right conditions—even without a pool and a handful of stones, you can enjoy the pleasures of the night.

Hooky Without Hang-ups

One morning my friend Harold called me at my office and asked, "What are you doing for lunch?"

"I'm free. Where do you want to eat?"

"Well, that's the point. How would you like to grab a sandwich and do something unusual? It's a perfect day for a movie."

"A movie? At noon? Are you crazy? I haven't the time."

"Look at it this way. If you go out for a normal business lunch, what time would you get back to the office?"

"Two, two-thirty."

"You meet me and I'll have you back by two-fifteen."

We meet at twelve and walk four blocks to a first-run movie I've been eager to see. "But I hate to wait in line," I tell Harold.

"You see, pleasure number one. No lines for the noon show. I can guarantee an almost empty theater."

He's right. There are only a few self-conscious businessmen inside.

"Most features run two hours," Harold explains, "and they all start at twelve or twelve-fifteen. You'll be back at your office before two-thirty. How often does that happen when you take a client out to lunch?"

"But that's business!"

"And this is pleasure. You have to learn to give the same amount of time to pleasure that you do to business."

Uncomfortably I look around the half-empty theater and notice that none of the other men is willing to meet my eye. Like me, they seem to have an uncomfortable feeling that they're doing something wrong.

"This is a fine idea," I tell Harold, "but I can't help feeling a little bit guilty about it."

"What you're doing," he replies, "is enjoying yourself during a time you have committed to an unhappy situation—work. You feel you're violating that commitment, but in fact you're only using your lunch hour." The lights begin to dim and he leans back and says, "Now enjoy. Here's the movie."

I'm able to banish my sense of unease, but when I get back to the office I have a sense of disorientation—for a few moments, things are out of joint. Then I have the sudden realization that I've put something over on my fellow workers. I've enjoyed myself when I wasn't supposed to.

Someone asks me, "What are you grinning at?"

I shrug. "I guess I just feel good."

Later Harold tells me, "That's a big part of the pleasure of movies at lunchtime—that feeling of putting something over on everyone else. I'm always ready to go back to work and put in a full afternoon because I feel that I've gotten away with something."

Since then I've become a firm believer in movies during the lunch hour. In the beginning I only went to those movies my wife didn't want to see. But one day, after I had told her about my midday pleasure, she said thoughtfully, "There's a new Altman film downtown, and I understand the lines go right around the block."

I shook my head. "Not for me. I hate waiting in line."

"Me too, but—maybe I could meet you at noon and we could see the first show?"

Agreed, and we did. The theater was half empty and we had our pick of seats.

"I feel as if I were doing something a bit wicked, as if I were on an assignation," my wife smiled. "There's something a little socially unacceptable about this!"

Settling down in the seat, I grinned. "We've got to get together like this more often."

I try to keep my noon movies down to two or three a month. Doing it too often would take away from the spontaneity of it. If I must eat, I pick up a sandwich and a container of coffee and feast discreetly during the picture. I can always get a seat by myself where the rattling of a brown-paper bag won't disturb my neighbors.

My only problem is that the fun is too much to keep to myself. I've turned a few other people I work with on to the pleasures of movies at noon, and now I'm losing that sense of "putting something over." I hope it doesn't detract from the pleasure. Then too, the other afternoon I found a group of young men and women giggling at the water cooler. It turned out they had taken in a porno movie during lunch. Now I wonder, Is this a whole new area?

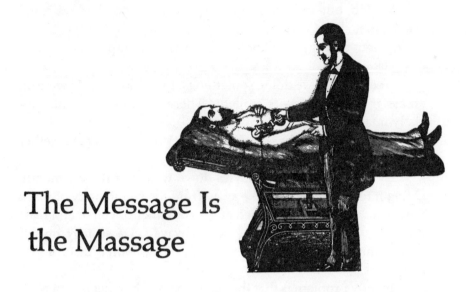

The Message Is
the Massage

I can trace my love for massage to my first severe attack of low back pain. Before that, the idea of anyone touching my body seemed an invasion of my privacy and somehow wrong. In my mind this intimate kind of touching was reserved for someone you loved.

A friend who was a recent massage "convert" brushed my objections aside. "It'll help your low back pain, sure, but massage is more than therapeutic. It's a source of pleasure."

I grimaced. "The idea of a complete stranger touching me turns me off."

"What are you afraid of?"

"I guess it's the bad press massage has gotten."

"Well, look—massage isn't a sexual act. It's sensual, sure, but basically it's a healing art. When I get a really good massage, it makes me complete, whole. How can I explain it? I get a message from the masseur's hands, and my body gives a message."

Convinced by my friend, I went to Marco, the masseur at my gym, and explained my problem—a spasm in the muscles of my lower back.

In a darkened room in a corner of the gym, I stretched out on my back on a padded table. Marco began by massaging my forehead, holding my head lightly with his palm for a moment, establishing a liaison of touch, then slowly and gently rubbing my forehead with his thumbs.

I wanted to remind him that the pain was in my back, but I decided to let him do his job in his own way. The darkness and the touch of his hands were having a strangely pleasant effect.

He slowly worked down my eyesockets, the balls of my eyes, my cheekbones and chin, then my ears, the back of my head and my neck and shoulders. He worked quietly and with rhythmic strokes, using a light film of oil to avoid friction.

My fears of being touched were minimized because he started with my head. But as he continued his hands seemed in part to massage, and in part to explore the contours of my body. A curious rapport built between us, a type of nonverbal communication that gradually eased the tension from my stomach, torso, arms, and legs until, when he finally reached my back, the spasm was much weaker than when he started. By relaxing every other part of me, he had relaxed these muscles as well.

Later, talking to Marco, I told him about my initial fears of being touched.

"That's very common," he nodded. "A lot of people have that fear."

"What do you do about it?"

"Well, usually I start with the back if I know the guy is uptight about being touched. Somehow, the back is the area where most people feel least threatened, in terms of being handled. With you, I could feel the tension all through your body, and I wanted to get as much of that out as I could before I got down to where the trouble really was."

The tension Marco felt in me was a muscle stiffening, a spasm. But it had been caused, as such spasms often are, by emotional tension, the pressures of work. By getting me to relax in the darkened room and by using a slow, gentle approach, Marco succeeded in draining most of the emotional tension out of me and brought the muscle spasm down to manageable proportions.

Since that day I've delved deeper into the pleasures of massage, and sometimes I refer to myself as a "massage addict." In fact, of course, there's no addiction involved; just a very deep sense of pleasure—provided the massage is done correctly. I realized the importance of technique the first time I took a massage when Marco wasn't on duty. His substitute had none of his expertise, and the experience was a total failure.

Marco has some definite views about massage and the pleasure you can get out of it.

"To be effective, massage should be received in the nude," he explains. "A darkened room and quiet are essential. I don't hold with music. It takes away from your concentration on the sensual aspect of the experience. While you're being massaged, center all your attention on your breathing and allow your thoughts to drift aimlessly.

"Let the masseur do the work. Don't help or try to help. Allow the sensation of touch to fill you completely and then there will be total communication on a tactile level."

Now that I'm a veteran at receiving and giving massage, I have come to realize how much the act of giving or getting it can make you aware of your body. This is doubly true if the person you are massaging, or who is massaging you, is someone you love.

Massage becomes a relationship between two people, the one giving the massage and the one receiving it, and it includes trust, empathy, and respect. If lovers give each other a massage, it's really beautiful, but that's a different experience, totally different.

Remember that in a very real sense we are our bodies. Anything that puts us in touch with our bodies also puts us in touch with ourselves. In our everyday lives we are very aware of our senses of sight, hearing, and smell—but we are less aware of our sense of touch.

Massage is an exercise in touching and being touched. It will help you to integrate touch into the rest of your life, to develop a tactile sense in relation to things outside your body. Through massage you can learn to get pleasure out of tables, chairs, eating utensils, stones, trees, and even the ground you walk on.

In body language, the unconscious message of our body speaks more truly than our words. In massage, this message is carried even further. Our voices are stilled, our eyes closed, and the language of touch becomes loud and strong. The massage becomes the message, and very quickly you learn the special pleasure of giving and receiving in the world of touch.

Love Is Green

Beth's apartment is cool and restful, the light from outside filtered through dozens of hanging plants that screen her windows like drapes.

"Do you know," she tells me, "Luther Burbank said that the secret of improved plant breeding is love. He often talked to his plants to show them his love."

"I find that hard to believe," I tell her.

"It's true. You know, nature intended us to live with green plants. It's no accident that the most restful color is green—our eyes evolved in the forests. That's the reason why I get such pleasure out of growing green plants.

"And it's a funny thing, but I enjoy my house plants differently at different times of the day. Like these spider plants. They're naturally graceful, but late in the day the shadows change them into something mysterious—almost like a tropical jungle."

She takes me to a southern window and shows me a glass

mobile hanging there. "When the sun comes in and hits this, it breaks the light up and reflects it in dozens of different ways. I see each plant a little differently when that happens."

She lifts the leaves of a huge fern. "I love any kind of fern. I raised this one from a little baby. They're hard to grow, but humidity and love help. Honest! Plants respond to me. They seem to know I love them, and they thrive on that love.

"One of the greatest things about plants is the flowers. Not all my house plants bloom, so every spring I plant bowls of bulbs and put them on the sills to mix with the green plants. I stick to narcissus because not only are they delicate and frail, but their odor fills the whole house, soft and subtle.

"You know, people enjoy visiting me, and I think a lot of their enjoyment comes from my plants. They give my whole apartment a good aura.

"I also get a tremendous amount of pleasure out of watching the plants grow. I don't like plants that never change. I take such delight in the new shoots and leaves."

She looks around the apartment and sighs. "I remember, back home, a spot near the house that's all green and mossy with a little creek nearby. I always feel recharged when I visit there, but I also get some of that feeling from my house plants, a revitalization. The smell of my plants is like the smell of that mossy little place.

"I'm always giving people cuttings from my plants. I feel that each time I do, I give a little of myself away—as if I sent a child of mine out into the world. I keep in touch with those plants and help my friends raise them.

"One of my greatest pleasures is coming home after I've been gone a long time. My feeling of home isn't based on possessions but on my plants."

She frowns a little. "I guess it has a lot to do with my love for the outdoors. The base of my pleasure is in bringing the outdoors inside. There's a sense of peace to this room because of the plants—the ferns particularly. They break up the light into such wonderful patterns. At night I set up candles so that the plants create shadows. That great big asparagus fern throws the most intimate patterns on the wall."

"Intimate?"

"Yes. Intimate and warm. It's especially wonderful while I'm making love. The shadows of the fern on our bodies give me a real high!" She runs her fingers down a frond of the plant. "Having plants all around you is a real luxury."

She nods at the corner where a dark-leafed plant grows in a wooden tub. "I've had that gardenia tree for three years, and it never bloomed till last month. Then one bud finally formed. When it opened it just saturated the room with its fragrance. Wow! I could feel its life force calming me, like transcendental meditation. I had to wait three years for it, but it was worth it—oh yes!"

The Snows of Yesteryear

"My grandmother was a fantastic sculptor," Lytton tells me. "She used to practice all the time with dough, making faces on cookies and intricate designs on bread and all kinds of lattice crusts on pies. But she was really in her glory after a heavy, sticky snowfall."

"What happened then?"

He smiles, remembering. "I can see her now. As a kid she seemed ageless, a shrunken, little old lady. She always wore buttoned-up boots and dresses to her calves. She'd put on a sweater and a scarf over her head and take a bread knife and a spoon with her into the front yard.

"My sister and I would help her roll snowballs across the lawn until they were at least two feet in diameter. Then she'd flatten the tops. We'd lift one onto another, put a third, smaller one on for the head, and she was in business."

"What kind of business?" I ask.

"We called it Michelangelo-ing. She'd consider the balls of snow for a minute, frowning a little, then she'd attack them with her spoon and bread knife, cursing all the while. The old lady had a seaman's vocabulary. She'd work like a fury, cutting and carving and shaping till she was breathless. Then she'd step back, and there it was.

"Sometimes it was a nude on classic Greek or Roman lines. Sometimes it would be an animal instead of a human, a polar bear or a seated lion or a seal. 'It all depends,' she'd tell us, 'on what's in the snow. Whatever's in there I'll let out. The important thing is, the snow must pack right. It has to be less than ice and harder than snow.'

"I used to admire her statues, but my sister and I really used to wish for an old-fashioned snowman—you know, three balls of snow with a broom and a hat and maybe a carrot for a nose, the kind everyone else made.

"When I'd tell her that, she'd shake her head. 'Anyone can make a snowman like that. Go ahead if it pleases you,' and she'd go back to her carving. Sometimes, when we were sure she had gone inside, my sister and I would roll extra balls of snow for our kind of snowman, the Frosty type."

I laugh and say, "But the pleasure of snowmen is more than just the carving of the figure, Lytton. It's the total ambience of a snowfall, of playing in the snow, of snowball fights and tasting the flakes on your tongue. It seems to me that when I was young we got much more pleasure out of snow. In the first place the snows seemed heavier. I remember the plows in the city throwing up such high banks of snow along the edge of the sidewalk—those banks were heavenly. We'd tunnel into them, make igloos and snow forts, and have wild snowball battles."

Lytton agrees. "It seems like that to me too. But maybe it was that way only one or two winters. You know, last winter a group of us went off to the mountains for a skiing weekend, but the snow came down too heavy and we couldn't get out on the slopes.

"In the afternoon we went into the yard behind the lodge and had a wonderful time in the snow. A group of us built a huge mound of snow, and I copied my grandmother's technique. We all carved and hacked and what emerged was a snow giant. Then we had a great snowball fight, chasing each other all around, and finally attacking the snowman itself.

"It's funny, it was then I remembered why we got such fun out of the simple ball-on-ball type of snowman with an old hat and a broom. When it was all finished we used to make an enormous pile of snowballs and take turns lobbing them at old Frosty to see who could knock off his hat first and then his head. We were such bloodthirsty kids!

"But you know, no one ever threw a snowball at grandmother's sculptures. We recognized that they were much too precious for that, or maybe we were afraid the old lady would come after us."

"Well, to me the snowmen were fun," I tell him, "and so were the forts and snowball fights, the wet clothes and freezing feet—but the best pleasure of all came afterward, when we'd sit in the kitchen drying out and drinking cups of rich, hot chocolate!"

Streams and Consciousness

"To me," Barry says thoughtfully, "the pleasure of fly fishing lies in its combination of intellectual and sensual elements."

I ask him to explain, and he frowns a bit, then says, "Fly casting is a very graceful act, if you do it well. When you build up a rhythm and accuracy, you feel that you're one with the river. You're out in a stream with waders, the water is rushing around you, and you cast. The very act of casting is slow and rhythmic. Your fly comes down and settles like a parachute on the water. It drifts with the current where you want it to, and you lift it off gracefully when you cast again.

"It's a slow-motion act, a sensual one, a fluid movement within a liquid environment." He spreads his hands. "Everything about it is sensual, especially the way the trout takes the fly—sometimes a delicate sip as if he were inhaling it, and sometimes a smashing, savage attack.

"There's that split second when you see the trout rise to the fly, and you feel an absolute physical tension. You have to exert tremendous discipline to keep from pulling the fly up. You have to force yourself to wait till he takes it, till the hook sets. It's a moment of exquisite suspense and pleasure!"

His eyes sparkle. "And then there's playing the fish. Another sensual act."

"You mean once he's risen to the fly and he's hooked?"

"Exactly. There's such delicate material between you and the fish. I mean the line. The test of a lead is often less than a pound, and a trout will often weigh more than a pound. When he's frightened, he has added strength. It takes a great deal of sensitivity and delicacy, knowing just how much pressure and tension to keep on the line."

Barry hesitates a moment. "You know, one of the real joys of fly casting is catching the fish and then putting him back in the stream, knowing you've done nothing to damage him. Don't get me wrong. It's not a sentimental feeling that fish shouldn't be killed. It's just—well, the realization that you can take something that nature has created, something fine and sensitive and beautiful, and use and re-use it for pleasure."

He laughs. "Hell, I've caught the same fish every day for a week. After a while it was like saying hello to an old friend. Some fish aren't too smart." He's quiet for a moment, smiling, then he says, "The point of not keeping the fish is that instead of depleting nature, you're increasing your pleasure."

"How is that?"

"Well, in a heavily fished, good trout stream where you always throw the fish back, most smarten up—not like my old friend. They become more wary and difficult to fool, so of course the pleasure of catching them is even greater."

"And the intellectual pleasure?" I ask.

He nods. "Yes, that too. You can't be a good fly fisher unless you've studied the entire environment of the trout. You have to know when he feeds, what he feeds on and how. Then too, you're not dealing with the fish alone, but with the entire complex environment where the fish reacts with hundreds of stimulants and conditions—the time, the insect population, the water, the weather, the temperature, the current—so many things.

"And there's the pleasure of achievement. When you catch a trout, you unlock a secret. Even if it happens over and over again the pleasure never diminishes. You know, in a sense, fishing a trout steam is dealing with a microcosm. Every day you solve a little more of the secret of existence and you come to realize how much there is about nature that you don't understand—but every bit you do learn is another part in a giant puzzle."

"And the environment is a part of the pleasure too?" I ask.

"Very much so. Just about every place where there's good trout fishing there is also great natural beauty. Part of the pleasure is the act of fishing, sure, but another part is the beauty of the surroundings. I can't separate the two. In every sense, when you're fly fishing, you blend into the environment."

He smiles. "I'll never forget one morning when I was fishing a small stream and instinctively felt that I wasn't alone. I turned and saw a doe, not ten feet away. She hadn't noticed me, maybe because I was so much a part of the environment, so in tune with the river. How can I describe the sheer pleasure of seeing her there?

"Or the pleasure I had in another stream where a bald eagle came to accept me. After a week of my fishing the same spot he just sat and watched me, not a hundred yards away. It was as if I had nature's permission to share his world."

"How would I go about learning fly casting?" I ask.

Barry shrugs. "There are lots of ways. If you're lucky, you might have a friend who's into fly fishing and willing to take you along one day.

"Or you can get advice from the stores. I picked up my first rod for a few dollars. I'd never seen anyone fishing. I asked the clerk in the store what equipment I'd need, and I went. It took me three months to catch my first fish! But I loved it. I'd stop people and ask, Am I doing it right? You learn. There are books, sure, but the best way to learn is by doing. Just wade in, literally, and begin to cast."

The Tiffany Touch

Margie collects antique art glass, manufactured around the turn of the century.

"I'll never forget the first time I was turned on to glass," she told me. "I went to visit a friend who had a fabulous collection. It was beautifully arranged in cupboards lit from within. When I walked into the room, it felt as if I were in a jewelry shop.

"She took out each piece and told me a little about it, how it was made and when, how and where she found it. She held each one up to the light to catch the iridescence or to show me the colors trapped inside the glass.

"I had seen glass before, but suddenly I had a new insight. I became aware that cameo glass could be multilayered, all blown together and etched and carved to give different colors and forms—such craftsmanship!

"I became aware of form for the first time, realizing that each vase matched form and design—a Gallé orchid on a low, squat bowl, a spray of iris on a tall, flaring vase. I saw pieces of Steuben glass so silvery to the touch, so rich in color—and Tiffany bowls and jars like woven gold!"

"Was all your pleasure in looking at it?" I asked.

She considered. "Part was in touching, too. My friend let me hold each piece, to sense the texture with my fingers. There's a tremendous tactile pleasure in handling glass. You want to hold it, yes, and look too, to put it up to the light. There's a doubly sensual joy in glass—it's tactile, but it's also visual. The color is locked into it, three-dimensional, deep, and changing.

"Once I began to collect glass myself, I learned that some glassmakers had found ways of changing the color as you looked into the glass. They produced one color on the outside and another within, both blending and shifting, a constant flow of motion in a solid medium. Sometimes they'd get the color to flow over the surface as it does in Tiffany's Favrile or Steuben's Aurene with the transparency beneath lending depth to the color. Seeing glass like that, touching it, owning it gives me a tremendous sense of pleasure."

"But surely," I asked, "you can go to a museum and see a collection of glass. Why do you have to own it yourself?"

"It's not the same in a museum," she said quickly. "There's another dimension to possession, to being able to pick a piece up at any time and handle it. You can always find new visual excitement in a piece of glass if you can handle it."

Thoughtfully, she added, "I had a piece of Nash glass once. Nash was a craftsman who worked for Tiffany. The piece had a surface iridescence of lilac and pink, but when you looked at the inside it was all a deep, deep blue. I could hold that piece and look at it and feel myself getting lost in its depths."

She smiled. "When you buy a piece of glass, you should feel an emotional attachment to it."

"But each piece is so expensive," I protested. "How can the average person collect it?"

"Settle for one piece. You can get a great deal of pleasure out of one beautiful vase or bowl properly displayed. The Chinese knew that. They would build an entire room around one piece of pottery or glass. Perhaps you get even more pleasure by simplifying the visual impact."

"How would I start collecting?"

"Go to someone you trust, a really reliable dealer. Shop

around and look and look. Keep searching and examining until you feel an emotional response when you handle a beautiful piece. It's a sense of deep, unalloyed pleasure. Then you're ready to buy, but only if you really, really want it.

"You know, you don't have to collect expensive glass. There is some very beautiful reasonably priced glass that can give you almost as much pleasure. But whatever range you decide on, get beauty and quality. Collect for pleasure, not investment. Buy intuitively. If you love a piece and respond to it, that piece belongs to you.

"I have a friend who collects damaged glass, cracked or chipped. It costs next to nothing, and if the damage is hidden, the pleasure is almost the same." She hesitated. "Almost, but not quite. Part of collecting is acquisition. There's pleasure in owning, and more in owning something valuable. It sounds a little immoral, but it's true. The true collector gets more pleasure when he finds something he owns has doubled or tripled in value!"

Beyond the Bikini

When sixteen-year-old Jennifer told me about the pleasures of skinny-dipping, my immediate reaction was, "But why not wear a suit? Isn't it just as pleasant?"

She tried to explain. "Look, suppose you get all ready to take a bath. You fill the tub with warm water, bath salts, whatever—then put on your bathing suit and ease yourself in. Does that make sense?"

"No, that's ridiculous, but—"

"Sure it is, but the difference between taking a bath with and without a bathing suit is a lot like swimming with and without a bathing suit."

"Well, one is private, the other is public."

She brushed that aside. "No, it's a matter of conditioning. We've been conditioned to associate swimming and a suit, though really, the bikinis today are only a couple of strings and a handful of cloth." She shook her head. "Even so, the difference between the skimpiest bikini and nudity is tremendous."

Jack, who's twenty-two, agreed with Jennifer. "The pleasantest experience I ever had, in terms of swimming," he told us, "occurred in the mountains in a small pond hollowed out of the shale by a tumbling waterfall. The water was cool and clear and it was surrounded by ferns and berry bushes. My friend and I came on it after a long, hot hike and we found half a dozen people swimming in the nude." He smiled. "We were actually a little annoyed. Should we go in anyway—God, that water looked inviting—or should we come back later after they had finished? While we were trying to make up our minds, one of the guys called out, 'Take off your clothes and come on in!'

"We only hesitated for a second. It was such a hot day, and we were all sweated up. We slipped out of our clothes and into the water."

"What was it like?"

"Well, for a few seconds we were vaguely uneasy. I guess we felt sort of vulnerable. But then our bodies relaxed as the water flowed over us. We swam for over an hour, diving through the waterfall and horsing around, sometimes with the others and sometimes by ourselves. There was no sense of nakedness, and yet we were completely naked. Is that contradictory? Let me see how to put it. We were aware of being naked on one level, a sensual level. There was the constant touch of the water, the freedom of our bodies—but on another level, a social level, there was no embarrassment. We were naked with strangers and they with us, but none of us was conscious of our nakedness as such. It was simply a pleasant way to swim.

"If I had to pinpoint the greatest element of pleasure involved," he said, "it would be the absolute sense of freedom, the buoyancy of the water plus the lack of any restrictive clothes, even the minimal restriction of a bikini.

"Then there was a sense of rightness about it—the trees, the rocks, the water and sky—all part of a natural system, and we, by shedding our clothes, had entered into that system. Nobody was hung up about not having a perfect body, being out of shape, or whatever—we just felt a part of nature.

"Another element of pleasure was feeling the cool water against every part of our bodies, particularly those parts we hold so private that we link uncovering them to a violation of our inner privacy. In that afternoon of nude swimming, there was no sense of violation, no sense of vulnerability."

I was deeply impressed by what Jennifer and Jack said, and I have taken their advice. I have skinny-dipped many times since, usually at night, and that I think holds the greatest source of pleasure for me. Any small whispers of uneasiness or self-consciousness are stilled by the enveloping darkness. The touch of the water combined with the touch of the night shields you and yet frees you.

I have gone skinny-dipping with groups of friends and have found not only a physical freedom in the feel of the water against my body, but also a social freedom in a mutually shared pleasure. It is amazing how many of our hang-ups are related to those last few square inches of cloth that we cling to like the old classic fig leaves.

I recall one wonderful afternoon spent with my wife on a deserted stretch of beach between dunes and water, where we both swam nude and found, along with our physical pleasure, a momentary return of a primeval innocence we had long forgotten.

That I am not alone in this choice of pleasure is proved by the growing rash of free beaches along the California coast, beaches where anyone can bathe in the nude.

Dr. Alex B. Comfort, in a foreword to a book about these beaches, says if people still swim dressed, it's because of the pressure of public morality. The true free-beach aficionado, he explains, undresses because he feels like it and scorns labels like nudism. Giving up one's clothes, he maintains, is a shedding of armaments.

In the travel section of the *New York Times*, Arthur S. Harris, Jr., a writer who spent a vacation swimming nude in the French West Indies, wrote that after a self-conscious first hour on the beach, he was caught up in the easygoing atmosphere of it all.

He stressed the sensual pleasure of the sun on his skin, and said, "Without clothes there on the sandy strip of Guadeloupe, we were free. We were of all ages and shapes—fat, slim, firm, sagging. We swam, sunbathed, picnicked, and simply enjoyed."

Looking Out

When I was very young—four, five, and six—one of my greatest pleasures was "looking out." We lived in a city, in a second-floor front apartment that overlooked a busy street. The windows all had metal safety guards bolted to the wood and bowed out to make miniature balconies.

When I wanted to "look out" my father would take a pillow and place it on the sill, propped against the guard, and then pull a low-backed chair up to the window. I'd kneel on the seat of the chair, lean my elbows on the pillow, and watch the street. It would keep me occupied for hours.

There was always so much doing, even on an ordinary day. There were a grocery and a shoe-repair store across the street, trolleys up at the corner, cars going past, and, in those days, horses and wagons. Ice was delivered by horse and wagon, as were milk and just about anything else that required a series of stops a few yards apart.

I could watch the children playing in the street, or the people passing. Sometimes, best of all, I could watch the other street watchers—the fat woman who spent most of the day sitting on a fruit box on the stoop across the street, or the grocer who stood in his doorway when business was slack and nodded at everyone who passed.

Part of my pleasure was simple voyeurism, seeing people go about their ordinary routine without being aware that I was up there watching. Part of it was trying to reconstruct the everyday interplays between people without hearing what they said.

When old Mr. Ryan, from down the block, stopped to talk to the grocer and waved his arms frantically while the shoemaker, known only as Dominick, joined in, what was it all about? Why were they so absorbed, so frantic when they interrupted each other? I didn't have to know. I could just watch and make up my own scenario.

Or when the fat lady stopped one of the neighbors and became involved in a long discussion. Why did they both laugh so much? From my spot above the world I could make up any answer to these intriguing puzzles.

I've never really gotten over the pleasure of watching other people. Sometimes I'll sit on a park bench and watch other sitters or walkers, intrigued by the vast differences between people. Hair, eyes, clothes—what a fantastic variety in clothes and the way they're worn!

Have you ever tried to guess a person's job by the clothes he wears or the way he walks? Try guessing personality from body language, or guessing nationality. Is there an Irish walk, a Scandinavian walk, a Spanish walk? Or watch a group of people talking. How close do they get to each other? How do they use their bodies?

Watch a group of men when a woman walks by. Watch a man alone when a woman passes.

Our park has a jogging track and it's great fun to watch the runners, to become aware of how differently men and women run, how every age has its own distinct running style, how weight affects running and walking.

Summer is probably the best people-watching time. People move more easily, wear more revealing clothes, and linger outdoors more. In winter everyone moves with determination, intent on getting from one place to another.

But whatever the season, wherever the place, I think the pleasantest people-watching is done when you, the watcher, are unnoticed, when you watch people move without restraint or self-consciousness. No watching has ever been as intriguing for me as those early "looking-out" days of my childhood, when, unobserved and unnoticed, I could kneel for hours and see life unfold on the street below.

Something for Nothing

"Look at that stove. It's practically new, and it didn't cost me a cent. A little polishing, and a few simple repairs here and there." Marty stands back in the kitchen of his summer cottage and admires his nearly new stove.

I examine it carefully. It's slightly used, but still in tiptop shape. "Where did you get it?"

"From the town dump!" he says triumphantly. "There's one section for garbage and another for appliances, stoves, sinks, cars, and other big stuff. I always stop there and browse a bit on my way out, and yesterday I found the stove. That family who bought the summer place on the hill redid the kitchen and tossed out all the old fixtures. I don't understand some people. That stove is in perfect shape. Why throw it out?"

"Well—you can't trade in a stove, can you?"

"Anyway, it's my luck. Boy, do I get a charge out of that. I could afford a new stove, but now I can use that money for something else. Come to think of it, I'm going back to the dump tomorrow. I've seen sinks there in great condition, and I want to make a bathroom out of that big hall closet."

"You sound as if you really enjoy the dump."

"I do. I get a genuine pleasure out of getting something for nothing, and I'll tell you—some of my neighbors have found fabulous things there."

"Like what?"

"Well, Norm up the road picked up a fourteen-foot diving board in perfect condition."

"Does he have a pool?"

"That's not the point. He also got a gas refrigerator in good working shape and a commercial double steel sink some restaurant had thrown away. You know, this is a throwaway society. It's amazing how little respect people have for objects. The minute something goes wrong, throw it out and get a new one. No one thinks of fixing anything. I've found perfect toasters with just one wire loose. Just three minutes with a screwdriver could fix it, and instead it's tossed out. It takes longer than three minutes to get a new one!"

"Not everyone knows how to fix things."

"They could learn. That's part of the fun, fixing up what I find. I found a whole mess of plastic containers in perfect shape. I washed them out and painted things like Tea, Coffee, you know, around them and I had a perfect set of canisters. There was a real sense of satisfaction in doing that, a feeling of accomplishment.

"And I have a friend who found a framed print at the dump. He was ready to tear out the print and salvage the frame, when he looked again and saw that the print was signed. On a chance he took it to the antiques shop in town and they gave him sixty bucks for it. Boy, there was profit in that pleasure!"

I'm amused at the pleasure Marty gets out of his freebies, and I tell my city friend Sally about it a few days later. She grins and points across her living room at a beautiful old-fashioned mahogany table. "How do you like that table?"

"It's a beauty. Where did you get it?"

"For free."

Startled, I look at it again. "There's no dump in the city. Did someone give it to you?"

"No, but on Friday morning the garbage trucks collect furniture in the city. If you want to get rid of something, you put it out on Thursday night. That's the night Jim and I stroll through the better neighborhoods, and your friend in the country is right. People throw out the darnedest things! This table had a broken drawer on one side. I put that side to the wall and it's perfect.

"I've picked up chairs and dressers—especially when we were first married and things were tight. You know, if I wanted to, I bet I could furnish our entire apartment from our Thursday-night forays."

"Do you like doing it?"

"I love it! It's like discovering a jewel where everyone else saw only pebbles. It's not only the joy of getting something for nothing, it's seeing something whose value nobody else realized. It makes me a little better than the rest. I see things from a different angle, maybe more clearly.

"Once someone had thrown away an old chest of drawers, and it looked awful, the paint all cracked and peeling. But I took a second look at it, and you know, it had great lines. I asked myself, I wonder what's under that paint? I scraped a bit off and it was oak, and not veneer, solid oak! I called Jim from the corner phone and we dragged it back to the apartment, spent a few evenings with paint remover stripping it down, and we ended up with a terrific chest. All it needed was new drawer pulls.

"Something like that is such a source of satisfaction to me. There's an almost creative accomplishment in it."

I thought of Sally's words a few months later when I was walking home on Thursday night and I saw a solid-wood packing case outside the local furniture store.

"Are you throwing it out?" I asked the owner, who was locking up.

He shrugged. "Sure. It's just a packing case."

But the wood was smooth and in good condition, and I needed bookshelves in my bedroom. I called my son, and we carried the case home, broke it up, and trimmed the long boards carefully. We got six beautiful four-foot planks out of it—and a tremendous sense of satisfaction.

"To tell you the truth," I told my son, "I feel as if I put something over on someone. I'm getting a terrific charge out of it."

"Yeah? Well, think of the trouble you saved the garbage collector. They'd just have to smash it up to get it in their truck." He looked thoughtful for a moment, then asked, "Hey, do you think people throw out radios and TVs when they don't work?"

"I'm sure they do."

"Now there's an idea. You know, there's a car dump near our college and we all go there to cannibalize cars for our own jalopies. Why couldn't I do the same with discarded TV sets, combine a few broken ones, and get a working set?"

"Why not?"

His face lit up. "When you come to think of it, if I keep my eyes open there should be any number of things I could put together, you know, like radios or stereo sets. I love putting things together."

"The possibilities are staggering," I agree. "You could get just about anything for nothing."

"Homes," he said suddenly. "My friend Dan hauled away lumber for nothing when he was building his place in the country—from wrecked houses. He did the wreckers a favor, and he saved the lumber to use on his own house—seasoned lumber, too. And I've heard that when they wreck buildings in the city, they'll let you cart away bricks if you want them. You just have to arrange it with the wrecking crew.

"You know, if I could apply the principle to food—I'd really have something!"

"There's always taxes."

"Well—no world is perfect."

May Your Days Grow Longer

"About ten years ago," Richard tells me, "I had it up to here with Christmas. I just felt that it had been commercialized to the point where it was ugly. Its meaning, its message—everything about it was perverted. Buy, buy, buy! It was no longer the season to be jolly, but the season to give the economy a boost, and advertising for it started right after Thanksgiving.

"The final straw came when I heard a commercial on my car radio, driving home one evening, to the tune of a Christmas carol! That did it. This year, I told my family, we're not going to celebrate Christmas.

"I took one look at my kids' shocked faces and realized what a boo-boo I had made. No matter how commercial it is, you can't take Christmas away from kids without giving them something equally good. Before they had a chance to protest, I had an inspiration. 'Instead of Christmas this year, we're celebrating the winter solstice,' I told the family.

" 'The winter what?' "

"Improvising as I talked, and desperately dredging some old stories of *The Golden Bough* out of my memory, I said, 'Christmas, Hanukkah, every winter celebration is a reconstruction of the original pagan holiday, the night of the winter solstice, the time of year when the days are shortest and the nights longest.'

"My ten-year-old asked, 'Why celebrate that?'

" 'Because,' I explained, 'as the days grew shorter, the pagans became terrified that eventually there would be no day at all—only night. So they had a wingding of a celebration to encourage the sun.'

"My six-year-old asked, 'What did they do?'

" 'They built bonfires on hills,' I said, 'to encourage the sun.' Seeing the sudden glow of interest in the three pairs of eyes, I added, 'Sometimes, today, it's hard to build bonfires, so we light candles and build fires in the fireplace.'

" 'And presents?' eight-year-old Amy asked hopefully. 'What about presents?'

" 'Of course there were solstice presents,' I explained, and as their doubts persisted I added, 'and pre-solstice presents and post-solstice presents.'

"That clinched it. My wife went along with it only, I'm convinced, because she wanted to see how far into a corner I could get myself.

"But to the surprise of both of us it worked out beautifully. We decked the halls with solstice decorations, golden suns and pagan trees and loads of candles of every size and shape, and the night of the twenty-first, solstice night, we lit them all. The house took on a flickering beauty that moved all of us.

"Oh, we kept Christmas as a purely religious experience, and my neighbor, who was delighted with the new holiday and shared it with us, kept Hanukkah, but we took the commercialism out of both.

"Once we had had a successful solstice, we began looking forward to the next one with all kinds of wild preparations. My neighbor organized a terrific bonfire with the fire chief's approval. My ten-year-old came up with a solstice greeting, 'May your days grow longer!' The answer, of course, was, 'May your nights grow shorter.' "

Richard laughs a bit, remembering. "We celebrated winter solstice for over ten years, and we still do. Part of the pleasure we get out of it is the realization that it's our very own holiday, and yet it's grounded in antiquity. Best of all, no one is promoting it or capitalizing on it. And, it's a natural holiday."

"What do you mean?" I ask.

"Well, recently I heard my eighteen-year-old telling a fellow natural foods freak, 'We were into nature years ago. We celebrate the winter solstice in our family, and it's a tribute to the basic forces of nature, a respect for the turn of the seasons, like we're in tune with the real thing that makes the world go round.'

"I was very moved to hear that," my friend Richard said.

Over the years, my own family has gotten a great deal of pleasure out of celebrating the winter solstice as a holiday. We've also experimented with the summer solstice, when the days are longest, and we've modified the old fertility rites to a sort of St. Valentine's day, but with more logic. We never had much luck celebrating the equinoxes, but recently I've acquired a number of grandnieces and I've tried them out with nonholidays, presents for nothing.

"Anyone," I told them, "can get a present on a birthday or holiday, but it takes someone special to get a present for no reason at all!"

They understood completely, and spent most of the year in anticipation of another present out of the blue.

We also borrowed from Lewis Carroll when our children were young and gave an occasional non-birthday party, an event that's impossible to anticipate, and so much more pleasant for that reason. We've also, from time to time, experimented with political and patriotic innovations. Inhouse Day (the day the flush toilet was invented), Step Day (the day American soldiers learned to march in unison), and any other apocryphal dates that were thought up—and many were.

Most were forgotten after they were enjoyed, but the best, like Solstice Day, have caught on and lasted.

Into the Third Dimension

"There was one time that was absolute, unalloyed pleasure," Danny, the scuba diver, tells me. "It was a perfect half hour. It happened on the California coast, south of Point Lobo, where I was exploring the underwater rock formations with a friend. I remember the water's color, a cool, translucent green. I knew my friend had wandered about a hundred yards away, but suddenly I had a feeling that I wasn't alone. I turned, and there was a small seal, about four feet long, practically touching me.

"Moving very slowly, trying not to startle it, I reached out and touched its belly, petting and stroking it. He didn't resist me, or seem at all frightened. After a minute he flipped his tail and circled behind me and then in front, and we began to play, the two of us. He'd swim circles around me, so graceful and free, and I'd imitate him clumsily. One time he let me put my arm around him for a brief moment, then he flipped away and circled back.

"We kept playing like that for a half hour, the most enchanting half hour of my life. All the trouble and time I had spent learning to dive seemed worthwhile for that brief time."

"Aside from moments like that," I ask after a pause, "what do you like best about scuba diving?"

"It's the most opposite thing to walking on land," Danny says quickly. When I look puzzled, he elaborates. "On land you have only two dimensions—front and back, side to side. In the water you have a third—up and down. That third dimension makes a fantastic difference."

Hesitating, he chews his lip. "How can I explain? You don't belong down there. Everything is different, even your sense of time."

"Time?"

"Yes. It seems slowed down. Your perspective underwater changes too. Maybe that affects your time sense. You have difficulty gauging the height of things, maybe because you're not fixed in one plane as you are on land.

"And then there's the movement. Underwater everything is alive and moving. The colors seem more intensified—reds, blues, greens, even grays. And of course there are the fish all around you, and the coral and rocks and sand—and plants, seaweed. They grow differently because of the water."

He shakes his head. "But the most marvelous things about scuba diving are the quiet and the enormous sense of peace it gives you. I told you about the motion of the fish and coral, but there's also the motion of the water, the currents pulling you back and forth. You can feel the surge and pulse of the sea, and there's a comfort to being a part of it.

"You have to rely on your sense of sight to get along down there. You can't use your legs for balance—there's a different set of physical laws for the scuba diver, and learning them is exciting. For one thing, they go against all the laws you've already learned."

"What do you need for scuba diving?" I ask. "How is it different from snorkeling, or just swimming underwater?"

"Well, you use a tank with scuba diving. It's a self-contained underwater breathing apparatus. You can stay down for long periods of time. You have fins on your feet to propel you along when you kick, a wet suit—a heavy rubber garment to keep you warm—and weights to overcome the natural buoyancy of your body so that you neither rise nor sink."

"Is it hard to learn?"

Danny shrugged. "It takes a few weeks to get to know the basics, and the best way to do that is with a thoroughly certified instructor. It's fun, but of course it can also be dangerous."

"Dangerous in what way?"

"Most of the danger is in panicking and forgetting what you know, or in not fully understanding the physics of diving. The body needs the same amount of air on the surface or below the water. The difference is in volume. You have to be aware of that and learn to descend and ascend slowly.

"There are all sorts of pleasures to be gotten out of scuba diving," Danny said, "but one of the greatest comes from using your body in a totally different way. There's a sense of freedom in gliding along as you watch everything about you. You have to travel slowly because you're in an unfamiliar world and you don't really belong. But because of the slowness, you see more going on about you.

"It's a place I don't really know, no matter how often I've dived, and I just can't take it for granted. Sometimes the water is clear and your vision is great. Sometimes it isn't so clear and you can only see a few feet. Your universe is suddenly pulled in around you, and you become very aware of that tiny area."

He smiles. "I surfaced once, after a couple of hours in water like that, where I could hardly see ten feet ahead. I lifted my mask to see blue sky and sun—and not ten feet away, a sea otter floating on its back and playing with a shell on its stomach.

"We looked at each other for about five minutes and then he turned and dove down, as if to say he preferred the pulled-in universe down there, where there was less chance of human invasion."

When No News Is Good News

"A few summers ago," Lila tells me, "Jim and I rented a cabin off in the woods. It was a great vacation, but we were so isolated. We had to drive six miles to get the daily paper. Well, that didn't last. We stocked up on groceries and just decided we'd do without the paper."

"It wasn't easy," Jim puts in. "I'm the kind of guy who's hooked on the news. I need my morning paper on the way to work, and my afternoon paper on the way home. Up there I had to do without my fix."

"We went cold turkey," Lila smiles, "We hadn't even brought a radio. For the first two days it was awful. We felt cut off and isolated, as if the world out there beyond the mountains had come to an end, and we were the only survivors. We began to think of excuses to drive into town, and then we'd realize that they were just that—excuses."

"But by the third day," Jim says, "we realized that something else had changed. The feeling of isolation left us—or perhaps it was just that by then the cabin was a familiar place. But we found that we were finishing breakfast, all of us, in a different mood, a pleasant mood."

"Really," Lila interrupts, "it was Jim who was different. At home he'd sit at breakfast reading the paper and shaking his head, growing furious with the government, this foreign country or that one, crime in the city, the recession, inflation, the national news and the international news—do you realize that there isn't any good news anymore? Or if there is, they don't bother to print it."

Nodding agreement, Jim says, "It's uncanny what going without a newspaper did for us. We spent three weeks in that cabin, and at the end of the first week, when we had to go into town for supplies, we both realized how much more pleasant life had become without newspapers. We decided to keep on like that, to see what would happen to us after three weeks of no news, good or bad—and, as Lila says, it's always bad."

"In town," Lila laughs, "Jim kept edging over to the counter where the papers were. I'd say, 'Jim!' very firmly, and he'd jump away guiltily. We went back with a week's supply of food and no news.

"It grew better and better. Both of us could feel the anxieties dropping away, and we realized that basically the news didn't matter. What difference did it make if we knew the latest headlines or we didn't?"

"Lila's right," Jim nods. "When I went back to work, I began the newspaper routine again, and it didn't matter that I'd missed three weeks. What had happened that wasn't always happening? The news was all basically the same."

"But what *had* happened," Lila said, "was three of the pleasantest weeks we've ever had. It was as if a cloud of gloom had been lifted. Maybe everything was just as bad as ever, but we didn't know about it—and we began to like and trust people again."

I thought a lot about Lila and Jim going three weeks without newspapers. Did it really give them pleasure? Then I had a chance to try it myself. I went off to one of the Caribbean islands on vacation and stayed at an isolated beach hotel—with no papers available. I missed them terribly for one or two days, and then I too felt the slow lifting of a cloud of anxiety that had always hovered over me.

Maybe the world was still hurtling toward apocalypse with tensions flaring in the East and the Western economy at the edge of disaster, the market in a shambles and crime rampant in the streets—maybe, but I didn't know about it. My not knowing didn't affect the world one way or the other, but brother, it affected me! The rest of that vacation had an extra edge of enjoyment to it.

I felt the same enjoyment during a newspaper strike, but then I shared it with the entire city and I swear the city came out of its horrors for a week. I also felt it on a trip to Europe by ship. Five days without a paper gave me the courage to avoid English papers during my two weeks on the Continent. I returned doubly refreshed.

Then the acid test. Could the same thing be achieved deliberately and consciously in this country while I went about my daily routine? Could I add an extra layer of pleasure to my life by omitting the daily carnage of the world and local news?

I tried it on a Saturday morning. Saturday papers are good to begin with. They have very little news in them anyway, but doing without the Sunday paper was rough. For one thing, I found myself with three extra hours of time and I became aware of just how much time goes into reading the daily and weekly papers. There are so many things I want to do, so much other reading I miss—the extra hours became a delight.

I lasted a week because that was the time limit I had set. I'm not yet ready to cut myself off from my culture completely. But for a whole week everything seemed lighter, a bit more optimistic, pleasanter—and I had the feeling I used to have when I was very young, that maybe the world and I would make it.

And a funny thing—none of my friends knew what I was doing. I was just as competent in my discussions of what was going on as before, perhaps because the exact same things went on as always.

Elementary Pleasures

"We were camping out, a group of us, and we decided to go into town to see a late movie," Elaine recalls. "We had cooked dinner over an open fire, and while the others were getting ready, I threw a few more logs on the fire and poked it around a bit.

"Then the others joined me and we sat there while it grew dark, just staring at the fire. At first someone said something about the movie, but no one made a move to go. It was just too pleasant there by the fire. Once in a while someone would poke it or put some more wood on. It went on like that till well after midnight. No one even mentioned the movie again! I think we were all kind of—bemused. You know what I mean. We were just hypnotized by the flames."

"What did you feel?"

"Staring into the fire? Oh, wow! I know I felt lazy, pleasantly lazy, and completely relaxed. The embers, the flames, the color —that orange-red against the black of the burnt wood—all seemed to ease away my tensions. I could have sat there forever, doing nothing but watching the flames. I wasn't a bit bored or restless. I didn't have to say anything or listen to anybody. I was thoroughly content to just sit and watch."

Fire watching, Elaine's pleasure, is as old as man's discovery of fire. There is something inescapably soothing about watching a fire, whether it's a campfire, a blaze in a fireplace, or a city fire in a can in an empty lot.

Wherever they are, flames are hypnotic; their lure is irresistible, their pleasure warm and comforting. It's as if all of your tensions burn slowly away.

"If I had to describe the softest, most relaxing, and laziest pleasure I know," Elaine says, "it would be stretching out on a rug in a darkened room watching a blazing fire in a fireplace."

"Is it the pleasure of watching?" I ask.

Frowning a little, she nods. "Yes. And you know, another deep pleasure is watching the sky when there are clouds."

"Just watching?"

"Yes. Lying on my back in the grass and trying to see things in the shape of the clouds. They change constantly, you know. One minute they're big puffy balls of wool, and then suddenly there's a dragon or a cat or a sailboat. You can see anything in clouds and then suddenly it's something else, or it's gone. The shapes change from second to second."

"Is lying on the grass part of it?"

Elaine frowned. "Not really. I once took a sunbath on an apartment roof. I watched the sky while I was stretched out there, and it was the same thing—the same tenuous shapes of clouds against the deep, bright blue, those crazy forms that suggest something you know, and then just as you see it, break up into something completely different. I can become almost as hypnotized by cloud watching as by fire watching."

"What about the third element?"

"You mean water? Fire, air, and water?"

"That's right. I remember a week spent in a friend's beach house in late October. The beach was deserted, most of the houses boarded up, and the air had the beginning of that bitter chill that promises winter. The living room of the house had a huge glass window that overlooked the dunes and the sea, and I would sit there for hours watching the water break on the sand and the rocks below, break and pull back and gather itself to tumble forward again—over and over endlessly, and yet every wave, every crashing pile of water, was different—unchanging, eternal, and yet always different!"

Elaine nods. "It's the same way with the clouds and the fire. Water too, but running water, breaking surf or a tumbling forest creek rushing over the rocks. I can sit watching it for hours and it's always different."

Fire, air, and water—the watcher's pleasures.

Getting It All Together

"I get a tremendous pleasure out of order," Shirley tells a group of us. "There are times when I'll take a load of laundry out of the dryer and spend a half hour carefully folding it. Just folding and piling it all up neatly gives me pleasure."

"But that's just a household chore!" I protest.

"Yes, and I hate housework—usually. But there's this extra element of order for folding clothes. Sometimes I get the same pleasure when I decide to rearrange my bureau drawers, or to sort out some of my possessions. It's as if, by sorting and organizing external things, in some way I'm ordering my own internal life."

"You mean it's a symbolic act?"

"Perhaps. I haven't thought about it that deeply. I just know that afterward I feel much more at peace with myself, more together."

I ask if anyone else has had the same experience, and Robert speaks up.

"I collect stamps," he tells me. "Sometimes I can sit for hours pasting them into my album, arranging and cataloging. It's one of my greatest pleasures, but, like Shirley says, a good part of it— maybe the greater part—comes from the sense of order I get out of a beautifully completed album. While I'm working at it, a rest-fulness fills me."

"I get that out of electronic kits," Tim put in.

I'm surprised at that. "Electronic kits?"

"Yes. Putting together a record player or a radio gives me the same feeling they're talking about. Look, I take a mess of ele-ments, and slowly and painstakingly I make order out of chaos. It's not the finished product that I'm after. I could easily afford to buy the record player or radio. Hell, it's only a few dollars more, and the time I put in is worth something. But there's an extra pleasure in seeing a logical, well-ordered structure come into being. I can be terribly upset, at my wits' end after a day at the office, and the tensions drain away. Or—wait a minute. No, it's not that they drain away. It's more like something inside me comes together as the project comes together. I pull all the loose ends of my being into a unified whole."

"When I'm upset," Carol says, "I cook. But I do it in a system-atic, orderly way. I take out my recipe and line up every ingre-dient on the table in little glass bowls. I like every step of the procedure to be well planned in advance. Then I begin. But I get the same feeling that Tim described. My tension loosens and everything seems to come together inside myself." She pauses, chewing her lip thoughtfully. "In a way, I suppose I get a similar pleasure out of putting the house in order. As Shirley said, it's an internalization of what I'm doing externally."

Fascinated by the group's experiences, I asked around among my other friends, and gradually I saw a pattern emerging. There is a very definite psychological pleasure to be gotten out of order. One man finds it in the business world by getting a company into shape, arranging the books and systems. Another finds it in construction.

"When I put a house up," he tells me, "I see a gigantic puzzle being solved. When the studding goes up just so, then every bit of wallboard and external sheathing fits perfectly. If you're six inches out of line you're lost. My kick comes in getting it exactly right, in seeing that every detail fits together. There's such beautiful logic to it all, such order."

Another friend who has a particularly chaotic job tells me, "When I get home I unwind by doing needlepoint. It's my secret vice, and nobody but my wife knows about it. I'll take half an hour before supper, and just setting out those ordered rows kind of ties up the entire day's frustration. I'm a different man when I sit down to eat."

I suddenly remember my own years as a puppeteer, when in the middle of the most grueling rehearsals I could sit down and methodically untangle a puppet's strings. As I brought the strings into order, I would feel the knots of tension inside me unravel.

The pleasure of achieving order, I realize, can be found on almost any level, and the more complicated our society grows, the more necessary it becomes.

The Wind in My Face

"I may get no kick from champagne," Iris says, "but I'll tell you one thing—riding high in the sky really sends me!"

"In a plane?"

"If it's an open plane. We were coming home from the country a few weekends ago, and we passed an airplane school that advertised rides in open-cockpit planes for ten dollars. I coaxed Bob into stopping and going up with me, and it was one of the most exciting rides I've ever had."

"In what way?"

"Well—if I had to sum it up, I'd say it was the sense of rushing through space, combined with the feeling of the wind against my face. It was just great!"

"Then it wasn't the airplane itself?"

She considers for a moment, then says emphatically, "No. It's the motion and, more important, the wind that please me so."

"But you can get that on a motorcycle."

She nods. "Another pleasure. I don't think I'd ever have married Bob if he wasn't a motorcycle freak. I don't even care about driving one myself. I never bothered to learn. I get my jollies out of hanging on and seeing the earth rush by, and again, it's the sensation of the wind against my face that turns me on."

"And the danger?"

"Oh yes, that too." She smiles. "Now that I think about it, it wouldn't be as exciting to me if I had to do the driving. Part of my pleasure comes from my being a helpless passenger, carried along at a fearful speed whether I want to or not."

"What about a roller coaster?"

"Oh, wow! That's the end, I love it. I love to sit up front in the first seat. Knowing that I have no control, that I'm just being propelled along in spite of myself, gives that extra little spice to it.

"I get it out of a convertible too, racing along the highway with the top down while someone else is driving—particularly at night. Then the whole world narrows down to the space in the car's headlights. We're in a little world of our own, tearing from nowhere to nowhere."

"Where else do you get it?"

She thinks a moment. "In a speedboat, again when someone else is driving. You see, I don't want to have control. I'd be too tense then, too concerned with where we were going, too caught up in driving the car or boat or plane. I want to be a passenger, but I want someone driving I can trust, so I don't have to worry about whether or not it's safe."

"What about skiing or surfing?"

She shakes her head. "They're not the same—they make me too aware of what I'm doing. I enjoy those sports, but they provide a different kind of pleasure, a controlled, aware pleasure. The pleasure I'm talking about doesn't demand any work or skill or concentration—just a feeling, a basic, almost primitive feeling.

"You know, sometimes I've stood on the top of a tall building, the Empire State or the Mark Hopkins in San Francisco, and I've had a brief fantasy of throwing myself out into space, with the air rushing past me—there's an excitement to the idea, but horror too because of the way it has to end. But on a motorcycle, in an airplane or a speedboat, I get the same thrill, and I know it will end all right.

"My pleasure isn't self-destructive, because even though the sense of danger heightens it, I don't, not for one second, want to be destroyed—at least I think I don't. That's why the pleasure is most intense when I can trust the driver."

She looks at her husband and sighs. "If I believed in reincarnation, I'd like to come back as a racing driver. That would be the living end!"

Feasting Alfresco

"One of the pleasantest lunches I've ever had," Neil tells me, "was in the park."

"You mean in the restaurant in the park?"

"No, no. It was a business lunch. There's a doctor I hire as a consultant for some medical advertising my firm handles. About every other month I take him out to lunch, usually at some over-priced French restaurant where the food is too rich, the liquor too much, and the noise overwhelming. I don't think either of us is wild about what we eat, but we do it in order to get together.

"We had a lunch date one beautiful June day, and I grumbled to my secretary about shutting ourselves up in a dark, noisy restaurant on such a glorious afternoon. She shrugged and said, 'Why don't you have a picnic in the park?'

"I laughed. Then I stopped laughing and thought, Why not? It's sinful to waste this weather. I called Dr. Simon, and he said okay, he'd bring a bottle of wine. Then I began to get excited. I stopped in at the Japanese import store at the corner and picked up a little basket, some plastic dishes, wineglasses, and some cutlery.

"In the fancy food store I bought a loaf of French bread, cheese, and fruit, and in the Syrian linen shop down the block, I picked up a checkered table cloth and napkins.

"We met at the park entrance like two kids playing hooky, and we wandered in until we found a grassy spot. We weren't the only ones. There were dozens of couples and groups scattered around, but I will say we were the classiest. We spread our checked cloth on the grass. Dr. Simon had brought a chilled white wine, and we filled our glasses and sipped while I cut the bread and cheese and unwrapped the fruit.

"We both took our ties and jackets off and loosened our collars. We sipped our wine and ate the bread and cheese and fruit lazily, watching a group of youngsters toss a Frisbee back and forth, hearing the laughter of other couples, and both of us felt utterly relaxed.

"We talked over our business casually but thoroughly, and then stretched out on the grass watching the sky, hearing the background hum of the city filtered through the park trees while life all around us seemed to slow its tempo.

"Later, reluctantly, we packed our stuff into the picnic basket and sauntered out of the park lazily. It was as if some spring inside had wound down. We had come in with all the tension of a business day, and we left at peace. Dr. Simon had office hours that afternoon, and he told me later it was the best day he had. 'I guess I carried the pleasure of that picnic right through the rest of the day,' he said, and I know I did!"

I've copied Neil's idea myself. I kept a picnic basket in my office with plates, cutlery, and wineglasses, and whenever the weather was right I took someone to a picnic. Sometimes it would be a business lunch, and in a way those were the best, probably because the idea was so unheard of to the people I took—and the results so pleasant.

Most of the pleasure of picnics, I believe, comes from winding down—from the contrast between the pace most of us lead and the comfortable, lazy calm of a picnic on the grass. The food should be simple, and if possible a cut above the quick plastic sandwiches and hamburgers we gulp at lunchtime, or the rich food we get in restaurants.

I've run the gamut from the checked tablecloth and chilled wine on the grass to the brown-paper bag on a park bench. Each type of picnic is pleasant, but the pleasure varies. It's most intense when everything is just right—a good wine, a perfect cheese, ripe fruit, fresh bread, and a glorious day. The pleasure stays with you for hours afterward, even days.

Of course there are bigger, more adventurous picnics, cook-outs at the shore or in the woods with the entire family. They're pleasant, but often the work involved, the cooking and cleaning and preparation, narrows the pleasure down to those few who have the least responsibility. Somebody has to start at daybreak and work like a Trojan if the large-scale picnic is to be a success.

The beauty of an office picnic, or any lunchtime one, is its impromptu nature. You can pick up the food at the corner store and nothing needs to be prepared in advance. The pleasure can be pure and unadulterated by any anxiety or tension.

Playing
the Game

The food was good, the hostess eager, but the party was just dull—until Moira arrived. Tall, good-looking, and with a charming English accent, Moira answered the inevitable, "And what do you do?" with a loud, "I'm an international tart."

The party picked up at once.

"Actually," Moira elaborated to a delighted audience, "I've been kept for the last six months by a filthy-rich oil sheik from one of those sticky little desert countries—I just don't dare mention names. . . ." Her wild story with its outrageous embroidery broke the ice, and in a few minutes everyone was having a great time.

Have you ever had the pleasure of telling a barefaced lie to a group of people and carrying it off to the point where half believed you, and the rest were delighted enough to go along with the gag? Moira does it to perfection, and my friend Arnold, who speaks a gibberish that sounds (to Westerners) exactly like Chinese and who has a vaguely Oriental face, has often kept a party in hysterics explaining Chairman Mao's works with the help of a knowledgeable translator.

There's a sure-fire icebreaking technique in this kind of zany playacting, but even beyond this, the skillful person who plays it perfectly straight can have a good deal of fun at even the dullest gathering. In addition, you can have the pleasure of role-playing—pretending, even for a few minutes, to be someone you aren't but would like to be.

I knew a young lady, Mimi, who had a lean, Slavic face and a tall, regal figure. After a few drinks—especially if the gathering was stodgy—she'd usually confess that she was one of the Romanoffs and would trace her ancestry back three generations, intriguing everyone with anecdotes about her family's escape from the Soviets. Her Russian accent grew thicker as the evening progressed, and one by one the guests caught on to the gag and even fed her lines.

The wonderful thing about Mimi, and what made it all so much fun, is that she never admitted that she was a fraud, even when she was caught in an out-and-out lie. She would wave her hand airily and dismiss all objections.

"Trifles, dahling, trifles!"

I sometimes thought she had become so caught up in the fantasy that she believed it herself, but whether she did or not, the fun began whenever Princess Mimi arrived.

Another variation of the *Barefaced Lie*, also guaranteed to perk up a boring event, is the *Indirect Lie*. For this you draw an innocent victim aside and indicate one of the guests. "Peter would die before he admitted it, but he's been hounded out of the C.I.A. for selling secrets to you-know-who. He's very sensitive about the whole thing."

Any doubt on the victim's part should be quickly countered with, "Well, let's forget the whole thing. I talked out of turn." Very few people can resist this bait.

When everything else fails, the *Crazy Sight Gag* may work. I knew a well-known comic who was magnificent at this. He and a girl friend would prepare their prop before the party—in one instance it was an elaborate hat with flowers and fruit, but some of the fruit, including a cluster of grapes, was real.

., At the party, the girl would sit down and get into an animated conversation while her escort would pass casually, do a quick take—making sure he had an audience—and then reach down and pick a grape and thoughtfully eat it, then another and another while the girl chatted brightly and seemingly unaware. I've seen at least three parties become hysterical affairs after this act, even when the whole routine was known by half the people. They waited breathlessly for the reaction of the others.

When the party is beyond rescue by lying or sight gags and must be endured stoically, there are still ways of extracting pleasure out of the other victims. A friend of mine plays a game with a make-believe camera. He and a partner will observe the gathering until there is one of those inevitable tableaus that should be preserved on film. Whoever sees it first will say "Click!" or "Gradget!" or some other code word they decide on beforehand. The object is to see how many "snaps" each can get in the course of an evening.

The pleasure in most of these games lies in the unexpected, catching your audience in something they're unprepared for, something blatantly outrageous or ridiculous. "I'm an international tart," "I'm John Wayne's stand-in," "I make my living as an industrial spy," "I'm testifying in secret before a congressional committee on sexual perversions on campus"—the variations are endless, and the fun depends on how much you can get away with before you're caught.

Hiding Out

"When I was seventeen," Rita tells me, "I ran away from home and went into hiding." Laughing at my surprise, she adds, "I didn't go very far or stay very long. Twenty-four hours, to be exact, and I left a note telling my parents I was visiting a friend."

"Were you?"

"No, I was in hiding. It's one of my favorite pleasures. When everything piles up to the point where I just can't cope, I go into hiding. That first time I was having trouble at school and a boy friend had just walked out on me. My family and friends were rubbing me raw. I had saved up about fifty dollars from babysitting, and I checked into one of San Francisco's very classy hotels—the Fairmont.

"I had a wonderful room overlooking the bay, and once I unpacked I took a long, leisurely bath, all scented and bubbly, then got into a caftan and ordered a fabulous dinner from room service."

"And you were all alone?"

"That's exactly what was so wonderful. I did my nails and sprawled on the bed with some movie magazines I had bought. I watched the late show and the late, late show on TV—I couldn't ever get away with that at home. And then I slept away the morning and had breakfast in bed—it was a real fantasy trip, the way Jean Harlow used to do it in the old movies. I just loafed away twenty-four hours, and when it was over I felt completely refreshed—one day was enough to do it, that time."

"You say that time. Were there others?"

"Oh, yes. I still do it when things pile up and threaten to overwhelm me. I just duck out, wherever I am, disappear, and check into the classiest, handsomest hotel around. Sometimes a place like the Fairmont in San Francisco is perfect—that is, the old part. The rooms are so large, the ceilings so high, there's such a sense of luxury. I could never afford it on a regular basis, but every once in a while I can revel in it.

"Once I checked into the St. Regis in New York. I was staying at another hotel with a friend—a very reasonable hotel because we were in New York for three weeks and we were making our money stretch. Then, halfway through the visit, I realized I had to get away. I had to be alone for at least a day, alone with my own body and the stuff in my head. And I wanted pampering. I don't know which I wanted more, to get away or to be pampered.

"Anyway, I invented a sick aunt out on Long Island and promptly checked into the St. Regis. I can remember the hot chocolate there so vividly! I had champagne in my room with my dinner. And I got up early the next morning, before dawn, and took one of those horsedrawn cabs for a ride in the park while the sun came up.

"It was so beautiful I cried—just heavenly. When I got back to the hotel I had breakfast by myself in the dining room. The table had snow-white linen and lovely crystal and china and a little rose in a bud vase. I only had toast and coffee, but it was so luxurious and perfect.

"Luxury is part of the pleasure, and so is pampering myself." She adds, "I guess it's just another escape, another way of leaving everyone behind. I put away all my problems, and just luxuriate in the lavishness of it all."

"Does it have to be an old hotel, like the Fairmont or the St. Regis?"

"Oh, no," Rita says quickly. "I've hidden out in new ones and had just as good a time. I've hidden at the Hyatt Regency in San Francisco with that fantastic lobby, and the Park Lane in New York, and there's a hotel in Dallas—I forget the name. Hey, a new hotel can be just as luxurious in a different way. That wonderful Miyako Hotel in San Francisco has sunken baths that are four feet deep and wide! They're sheer heaven." She spreads her hands. "It's all self-indulgence. That's the key."

"Do you ever hide out for longer than a day?"

"My limit is twenty-four hours." Very seriously, she explains, "You see, if it's for one night and at rare intervals, I can afford just about any hotel in the world. If I stayed longer I'd worry about how much I was spending, but a one-night stay, even with room service and all the extra goodies, rarely comes to over a hundred dollars, even in the most posh place. And it's all the more intense because it's only for a night. You don't get a chance, not for one minute, to get bored.

"Oh, I've done it sometimes when I have some extra money to play with, but most often I do it when the situation is bad, when things are closing in and I have to get my head on straight again. It puts everything back into perspective, and it refreshes me absolutely!"

Sharing the Symbolic

My Japanese friend Margaret attended a Passover seder with me, and afterward I apologized for what I felt was an interminable service. "It must have bored you stiff."

Her eyes sparkled. "Not at all! I loved every minute of it. It's a wonderful ritual, full of such great symbolism. The bitter herbs, the egg in salt water, that ground stuff with apples that tastes so sweet, what is it? Haroseth?"

I nodded, and she went on. "It symbolized the mortar in the bricks they used to build with in old Egypt. It just blew my mind—it's all so fascinating." She hesitated. "It gave me a sense of timelessness. It was as if everyone at the seder—even me—as if we were all connected to the past by invisible threads. There was a feeling of togetherness, of sharing. I just don't think I could put all the pleasure it gave me into words."

"But you have your rituals too."

"Oh, yes, and I love them. I love our tea ceremony back home, dressing in beautiful kimonos, the color and texture of the cloth, of the mats on the floor, of the walls—and then the ritual of pouring, the symbolism of the cup as humanity. It fills me with a sense of calm, of communion, the same sense I felt at the seder."

I remembered Margaret's words a few months later. I had been invited to a small formal dinner with my wife. I grumbled while putting on my evening clothes, but when she was dressed my wife smiled up and said, "Don't you love it?"

"Getting dressed up?" I asked in surprise.

"Yes. That and the dinner itself. Everything will be fancy like our clothes—the linen, the table setting, the food . . ."

Thoughtfully, I said, "It's kind of a ritual. Isn't it?"

"Oh yes, and that's why it's such fun. You'll see."

She was right. The candlelight, the other women in their beautiful gowns, the men in evening dress, the exquisite service —all seemed part of a very old, established ritual. I remembered Margaret's tea ceremony and thought, "How similar it is!" There was a correct protocol, the same type of visual beauty, and a similar symbolism.

I have found that same sense of ritual in many things, and each time it fills me with pleasure. Certain church services, communions, bar mitzvahs, baptisms, masses—all fall into this category.

I remember, as a child at a summer camp, a Friday-evening religious service out in the open under a row of apple trees. The words from the Psalms, repeated by all of us, were more meaningful out there with the mountains and trees around us. Again there was a sense of ritual, the tie with the past, and the communion with the others moved me.

Religious services are all deeply ritualistic and filled with symbols, yet pleasant to sit through. But there are simpler, no less pleasant rituals that all of us share on a daily basis. The ritual of our evening meal is one.

"We rush through breakfast," a housewife told me recently. My husband is in a hurry to get to the office, the kids tearing to make the school bus, and I'm eager to get the housework over with. I load the dishwasher while they're wolfing down their toast and tea and milk and all the rest.

"Lunch isn't any better. I grab a sandwich on the run, resenting the few minutes I give up to eat it. There are a dozen things I'd rather do, things I must do.

"But dinner"—she smiled and sighed—"now that's a different setup altogether. I won't let my family eat dinner on the run. We all have to sit down together, and my husband says a little benediction—we're not religious, but we like—well, the quiet it brings. I like to set the table nicely, and I serve slowly. We eat and talk and it's a time we spend together, a social time."

Dinner was that family's ritual, something each of them would look back on with pleasure. Most of us have some small ritual we use to pleasure ourselves. Sometimes we perform it once or twice or a few times a year. Others repeat the ritual as often as the Japanese do their tea ceremony, and a few, like my friend, have it on a daily basis.

Zen and the Art of Golf

"To me," John says, "pleasure is a transformation in consciousness—and golf is that sort of a conscious-transforming experience."

John is a doctor of philosophy and an ardent golfer. "Is that the basic pleasure in the game?" I ask.

"Oh, there are other pleasures—the physical environment, the fresh air and the grass and the dirt—you know, golf courses are so well manicured that even the dirt is clean. But those are minor pleasures. What I consider the greatest pleasure in golf, perhaps the basic pleasure, is the *moment*."

"The *moment?*"

"What I call the *moment*. Let me approach it by talking about consciousness. To me, consciousness is a differentiating factor. I look around the room and use consciousness to separate the lamp from the table, from the chair—our lives are filled with different objects.

"Golf can be a means by which the consciousness gets beyond this fragmented view of the world. It can restore a unity to our experience."

"But how?" I ask in bewilderment. "What has this all to do with golf?"

"Let me give you an example," John says. "Here is the golfer, with his ball and his club, on the golf course. Each of these things is separate and can be analyzed. But when I stand over the ball, all these things cease to stand apart. They melt into one another, blend into a whole, a unity."

"A little like a Zen approach." I am half joking, but John takes me seriously.

"A lot like it. You can speak of Zen and the art of golfing and not be far off, but I think of golf as a transcendent sport. It transcends the normal way consciousness works."

Still puzzled, I ask, "How?"

"By restoring a unity," John explains. "The system comes into play as I prepare to hit the ball. My thinking about things slowly comes to a halt. I'm not thinking at all, but I'm not in a state of blank unconsciousness. There's a curious alertness, a readiness."

His eyes glow as he talks, and I begin to understand what he means. "You see, a system is slowly created and in those two or three seconds, what I think of as the *moment*, from the time I feel absolutely ready to hit the ball until I lift up my head and see the ball fly—those few seconds contain for me the really extraordinary pleasure of golf."

I nod, and he probes a bit deeper. "There are three steps to the *moment*. One is the emptying of consciousness, and I achieve this by focusing on the golf ball—just looking at it, using the ball to center my vision. By concentrating on it, I shut out everything else.

"Step two is a slow merging of consciousness and nature. I no longer experience myself as different from the world, but instead I'm a part of it, of everything around me.

"Step three is the impact of the golf club and the flight of the ball itself. In that graceful parabola I see a symbol of the conquest of everything earthbound and inert."

He gestures. "That soaring ball even laughs at gravity for a few seconds!"

Embarrassed now, he laughs. "That's it in a nutshell. Golf, you see, is only a means to that *moment*. I suppose archery or billiards or—oh, so many other sports might be the same."

He interrupts me as I start to speak, anticipating my question. "There's one thing, of course, a prerequisite for experiencing that *moment* to the fullest, and that's skill. You must be extremely skillful at the game. You can only reach that emptying of consciousness and merging into nature if you're so good, so expert, that your motions are automatic.

"The body must function to the point where the play is, well, instinctive. Not intellectual at all. Look, when you're practicing you concentrate on holding your left arm straight, transferring your weight properly, keeping your head down—all those things, and more. But when the *moment* comes, you don't think of those things at all."

"Does it always come?"

He shakes his head. "That's just it. You can never depend on it. Sometimes, no matter how you practice, something goes wrong."

"Is it the first drive on each hole that counts?"

"Oh, no. The *moment* can come with a 250-yard drive, sure, but it can also come in a five-foot putt or a twenty-yard pitch shot. The essential thing, if the *moment* is to come, is that the body and mind are attuned.

"You have to be able to empty your mind till everything about you stops. When the mind reaches that state, the body automatically knows it's time to swing." Again he hesitates, nodding slowly. "You know, the feeling of pleasure I get is serenity, peacefulness, wholeness—and even health. I'm at the center of experience. It's a beautiful feeling, intellectually beautiful." He laughs self-consciously. "I guess it's the penultimate in getting away from it all.

Slow Motion for the Auto Age

Tim is a bicycle freak, and he'll take his ten-speed out at least once a day to do some twenty-odd miles. "I really dig it," he tells me. "It's my chance to be alone, to get away from things, out in the open—it's the way I get it all together."

"You could do that with a car."

He shakes his head. "It's not the same. With a bike, my own power is moving me. I have to work to get where I'm going, and I end up with a sense of accomplishment. And then, too, I see the world from a different perspective."

"What do you mean?"

"Well—you move more slowly and you have time to notice little things, like wildflowers at the side of the road. They're only a blur when you pass by in a car. And animals. It's a quieter world when you ride a bike, and animals aren't scared away. I've seen badgers, raccoons, beavers, rabbits, turtles, squirrels, chipmunks, deer. Once I saw a bear! You may never realize how full of life the world is, how many animals there are even a few miles from civilization."

He laughs. "And, of course, dogs! But they're a minus, not a plus. For some reason cyclists are perfect targets for dogs to run after and bite. You could call them a challenge, I guess.

"But people. Wow, they take a different attitude when you bike past. I don't know why. Maybe they see you as less of a threat than when you're in a car. The point is, everyone likes a cyclist. People are a little nicer and a little friendlier to us.

"Speaking of friendliness, I've never met an unfriendly cyclist. That's part of the fun too, the other cyclists you meet. They're always ready to rap and swap stories. Maybe it's because you both have that bike and all its problems in common."

"Are there many problems?"

"Oh, sure, but they're fun. You know, a bicycle is a great machine. It can be very simple, and also very complex if it's a ten-speed. Still, almost anyone can learn to take it apart and put it together, and that's part of the pleasure—making it work a little better when you get it back together."

Shaping a hill with his hand, he says, "Take topography, for instance. We all know about it, but driving alone in a car you ignore it. You step a little harder on the gas when you come to a hill and your car zooms up. Not with a bike. You feel that hill. You know it's there. It's sheer work to get up it and a wonderful pleasure to come racing down with the wind in your face—oh, man!

"But even little hills, the kind you never notice in a car, are obvious to a cyclist. And that's another pleasure—the realization of just how wrinkled and up-and-down this world is.

"And weather! I've been out in a drizzle and in a rain. I've biked when the sun baked down at me, and when it was so cold I had gooseflesh. You can bike in almost any weather, but the important thing is that you become aware of the weather like you never are in a car, or even walking, when you can take shelter. Sometimes I wonder why I go out in some of the storms I ride in, except—well, it's fun. It's a different sort of pleasure to feel—to really *feel* the weather."

"Do you always bike alone?"

"Oh, no. Of course it's great to get off by yourself, but it's also fun to go in a group. Then there's an added element, the sense of helping each other, a companionship of the wheel. Bicycling isn't a competitive sport. Oh, sure, when we ride in a big group a few of us will usually pull ahead of the others. But that's a matter of pacing, riding at a speed that's comfortable for you even if it's faster than the group. Group cycling is as much a pleasure in its own way as riding alone.

"Still, to me—and this of course is a matter of taste—getting away alone is the great part of cycling. When I'm wound up, tight, under pressure for weeks, I can get out and unwind just by pedaling. There's a joy to the sheer exercise of it. And I feel great afterward. You know, once in college I had pulled an all-nighter, studying till six in the morning. I was zonked out, but I took my bike out and pedaled twenty miles! Do you know, I felt fantastic afterward. My feet and legs hurt, but I was psychologically satisfied and relaxed—and that sunrise! Oh, man!"

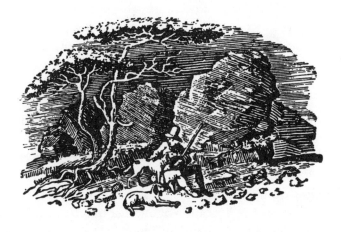

The World Forgetting

A friend of mine who does documentary films was traveling by plane across Alaska to the Arctic.

"Our jumping-off place was a small valley at the edge of a glacier," he told me. "We were to begin our trek north from there across the ice on foot. Arrangements had been made with a priest who lived in a small hut on the valley's rim. He was to put me up while the plane returned to the base for additional supplies and the camera crew.

"I was to stay with him overnight, but bad weather delayed the plane, and I was alone in that hut with Father Vishnikoff for a week. He apologized at the beginning and explained that he was accustomed to silence. I promised not to interrupt his routine, and we both agreed to go our own ways. He had some small chores, none too demanding. I had nothing to do but become more and more aware of the overwhelming solitude of that hut on the edge of the glacier.

"At first it was pleasant, a chance to unwind—for the first eight hours or so. Then the silence became harder and harder to take. I was determined to respect Father Vishnikoff's needs—after all, I had been wished on him—and I kept to myself. But more and more I became aware of the terrifying, overwhelming solitude all about me. For three days it was dreadful, and then on the fourth I realized that I was no longer lonely. I was alone, but I felt no desire for company. I found that without consciously trying I was avoiding the priest.

"What did I do in those last days before the plane came? I ate my meals with Father Vishnikoff, but in silence. After dinner he would light up a pipe, and I'd smoke one of my store of cigars. Perhaps that was the best time of all, just quietly sitting together, not talking, yet in a peculiar way communing.

"During the day I would take long walks out onto the glacier or down toward the valley. The hut was built on barren, rocky soil midway up the mountain wall. A few miles below, there were stunted trees and bushes, but at the level of the hut there were only boulders and the looming glacier. Sometimes I would sit for hours, watching the mountains, the sky, the massing clouds, and the long sweep of barren ground that led to the green far below.

"When the plane finally came I was glad, and yet disappointed. Something had filtered into me from the solitude all around, a sense of peace, of calm, of intense quiet. I said goodbye to Father Vishnikoff reluctantly, and he politely urged me to return, but I sensed he felt a deep relief that I was finally going and he'd be alone again.

"My crew was sympathetic about my long stay, and one of the cameramen said, 'Christ, how did you take a week there?' Looking back at the hut from the glacier, I shook my head. 'It was very easy,' I told him. 'What was hard was fighting the temptation to stay on!'

"Since then I've tried to recapture that feeling of solitude. I've succeeded a few times, but only when I've been alone. Once in a cabin up in Maine in the autumn, I was by myself for two weeks. Again it took a few days before I felt that same satisfying sense of rightness. I don't remember what I thought about during those weeks—or if I thought at all. I just know I was at peace."

I've also tried to find the inner pleasure my friend got out of solitude. I've spent a week alone at the beach in the early winter, and another week at a friend's cottage in the mountains. Both times I found the first day the hardest, but while it took my friend two or three days to experience the pleasure of solitude, it only took me a day. Then, whether in front of a fire or walking a deserted beach or a solitary trail through the woods, I've experienced that same inner tranquility, that unwinding calm—the extreme pleasure of solitude.

Another friend smiled when I told her of this.

"You don't really need your cabin or seashore or mountain retreat," she said. "I close and bolt my door, turn off the phone in my apartment, and lower the shades and drapes to shut out the city, and I find the same pleasure in a matter of minutes. The reason it takes you so long is because the conviction of solitude, the realization that you are alone, must first sink in. You feel a momentary panic when you realize just how isolated you are, and then you can relax and enjoy it.

"I don't experience that panic sealed up in my apartment. I can break my solitude in a moment, and maybe that's why I can enjoy it so quickly—and, Lord, I need it. Sure, it's a pleasure, but it's more than a pleasure. Being alone, without a book, newspaper, radio, or telephone, revitalizes me!"

Seeing the Sensuous Rainbow

"One of the most far-out things that ever happened to me occurred during a ride on the freeway one evening," my friend
Chris, the painter, tells me.

"In a car?" I ask.

"Yeah. I was driving, alone. It was winter, late in the afternoon,
and there was snow all over—everything was white except the sky.
That was a light salmon pink, but very subdued. Man, it was just
so peaceful and quiet, I just flipped. The pale-pink sky, the
snow—I was just lost in the color of it." He pushes back his hair
and strokes his beard. "Wow!"

"That's a funny way of putting it, lost in the color of it."

"Well, yes." Chris smiles and leans back, stretching out his
legs in paint-smeared jeans. "But it's true. There are times, you
know, like after a storm, when the earth and the sky and the air are

all"—he frowned, searching for the right word—"lucent! That's it. Green and lucent, and the whole world sort of forces you to notice it. At times like that I'm just overwhelmed with color. You know, color itself becomes another dimension, a fourth dimension that exists all around us."

I nod, trying to think of similar moments I've experienced—sunsets, early-morning walks as the sun rises, a deep dive in a tropical ocean, a beach at midday.

"Is it always a function of nature?" I ask.

We're sitting in the living room of Chris's apartment in the late afternoon, and he points out the window at the darkening blue sky.

"Sometimes," he says. "But look at the brown wood of the window frame and then that intense blue of the sky against it. You see what the brown of the wood does to the blue? See how it deepens it and makes it stronger? I can look at that blue and brown and it just blows my mind. You know, the pleasure you get out of color is more than just looking at it and saying, That's a pretty rose. That's a nice shirt. You have to understand that the colors change according to what they're against. That rose is fantastic against the violet couch. That shirt is exciting when your skin is brown, or when you have blue pants on. What I mean is, one color reduces or changes or exaggerates another. That blue sky against the brown wood, wow! But if I were out of doors the blue would be different, maybe sad, lonely—but different."

Scratching his beard, Chris says, "To me color is something I can feel as well as see. Like, when people cry I hear them, but I also feel them. I feel that they're hurt. Do you dig me?"

I nod and he continues earnestly. "I look at colors and I feel the pressure of one against the other. That blue sky is brilliant against the brown, but I could make it cry by putting it next to a warm gray, or an orange—yet the blue is still the same."

"And each arrangement affects you?

"Oh, yes. I feel colors in a sensual way. They turn me on. When you can experience color like that, you begin to see the world, really see it. You know, I was driving over a bridge one afternoon, and suddenly the red iron of the bridge, the gray of the water, and the sky, the sun, oh, wow! All of that color just overwhelmed me. I began to cry. I wasn't sad or anything, but I know I was feeling that color so intensely, so privately, that I had to cry."

He frowns, clenching his fist. "Color is a world of its own. It's outside you, maybe alien to you, but it's still something you want to absorb. When I see a sunset, or the white light of the sun at midday, I want it to fill all the pores of my body. I want to drink it in!

"And I find color everywhere. In clothes. On the covers of books and magazines. It's not just in nature, but there's color in a rose, the sky, trees . . . It doesn't matter where I see it."

Excited now, Chris says, "Look, the thing you must do to get pleasure out of color, to really feel and enjoy it, is forget about the literal thing. I mean, forget what a thing is. Just see form and color, but see it against a background.

"You know, even now I can get a charge out of things I remember. When I was backpacking in Europe, there was a pink and red house in Luxembourg . . . I remember a green storefront in San Francisco, a yellow field of hay in Ohio . . . The world, to me, is splashes of color in my memory."

He pauses a moment. "You know, the hardest thing is to break away from what you know, from what you've been taught to look at, to look for. Like most people only see color in terms of the object it's on. A red car, a yellow pot, blue jeans . . . But you have to get beyond that."

Biting his lip, Chris is obviously searching for a way to make me understand. Suddenly he says, "What you can do is squint, you know? Narrow your eyes so that everything is out of focus and you can't distinguish what things are. Then you can separate the object from its meaning, destroy the literal object, and see only the color. You dig that? By closing your eyes a little you're really opening your sight!"

Instant Party

"I remember a story my dad told me about World War II," Rod says. "He was waiting for a train at Penn Station, and there was a line-up outside the gate with the usual number of servicemen saying goodbye to their girls. There was this one couple, he told me, really going at it hot and heavy, a goodbye kiss to end all goodbye kisses—except that when the gate opened and the line moved onto the platform, the sailor and his girl strolled over to another line and went into another embrace.

"Funny. That story really gave me a charge, and about a year ago I was out on a date with a girl and we had no place to go." Rod laughs. "I had a brainstorm. Why should only sailors say good-bye? There was a bus station in town, so we drove over, went into the waiting room, and joined a line. There were a lot of college kids going back to school, so we weren't alone. We had at least six warm, intimate goodbyes, both of us giggling like crazy and fighting to keep from breaking up.

"Since then I've tried all sorts of variations on the same theme. I think my favorite is going down to the docks when the cruise ships take off. There's a real party atmosphere, and there should be. The ship is full of farewell parties. You have to pay a dollar to get on to the ship, and then you can mingle with the tourists and their friends. I've crashed so many shipboard parties I've become an old hand at it. Everyone assumes that you're someone else's friend.

"Sometimes I pretend that I'm on the cruise too, getting ready to take off. Sometimes I'm seeing someone off but I can't seem to find him. Usually, I'll barge into a party going full blast and I ask if Shirley's here yet. If people get uptight about it I'll shrug and say I must have the wrong room number, but half the time someone will shove a drink at me and I'm part of the celebration."

Rod grins at a sudden memory. "One time on the *Sea Venture*, a big cruise ship, I crashed one of the parties in a lounge and pulled my usual routine of asking for Shirley, and this good-looking woman comes over, half loaded, and throws her arms around me. 'I'm Shirley!' she yells out. Wow, that turned out to be a great party. I even took Shirley home."

When I told my friend Al about Rod's party-crashing, he nodded.

"Basically, you know, Rod's a beginner," said Al. "I mean, I've been crashing parties for years. It's far out, but the best place to crash isn't a ship. It's a big hotel, especially during a convention. There are dozens of big cocktail parties going, and no one's going to insult you by asking for identification.

"I got into crashing when I stayed in a hotel in Chicago during an American Medical Association convention. Some drug company had hired a suite on my floor and I wandered in by accident. Man, before I could get out someone had given me a drink and I was part of the scene. I had sense enough to keep my mouth shut and listen and I had a great time, beautiful!"

"So you tried it again."

"Sure. I began looking for parties after that. You know, they're all posted down in the lobby on bulletin boards. I went to six parties during the Chicago trip, and since then I've done it in my own home city. Anyone can do it. Just wander into a big hotel, check the board for affairs, and go right up. Hey, I've tried bar mitzvahs and weddings!"

"Doesn't anyone stop you?"

"Oh, sure, every now and then. So what? I just say Alex or Sam or someone invited me. At conventions you're expected to have a badge with a name tag, but no one checks up. They're all afraid to embarrass you by asking. Just say you forgot it. Half the people don't wear badges anyway."

"And you aren't nervous? I'd be scared to death."

"At first, I was, but now—what the hell. If I'm found out I confess. What can they do? Throw me out? The point is I meet all kinds of really beautiful people. I've rapped with the greatest guys and gals. I've been to teachers' conventions, engineering, medical, legal. When you're bored or lonely, it's the greatest.

"And lately I've graduated from hotels. I was visiting a friend and there was a wild party going on next door. She kept saying, 'I ought to call the super,' and finally I said, 'If you can't lick them, join them!' So we just walked in, and within an hour we'd met a whole new group of great people.

"The funny thing is, no one wants to know you're crashing, even if they suspect it. They'd much rather think you were someone else's friend, and if you pretend you are, no one's about to call you."

He sighs. "I'd love to get into some society parties. It takes real nerve to try it, but I'm getting up the guts. Meanwhile I practice on smaller affairs, and it's amazing how large my circle of friends has become. Last week I crashed a party and found that I knew half a dozen of the people there from other parties I'd crashed!"

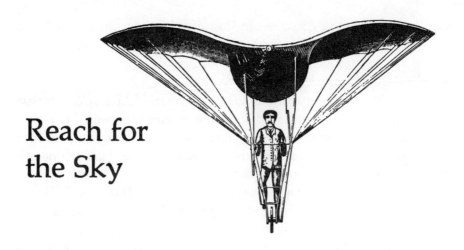

Reach for
the Sky

I meet Carl at his office to talk about soaring. In his thirties, slightly overweight and tightly wound up, Carl paces constantly as he talks. When I ask him about his glider, he corrects me quickly.

"The proper term for what I fly is a sailplane, not a glider." Flying a sailplane, he explains, involves much more than just gliding. "With a glider, you're towed aloft and you glide down. Soaring involves staying up and even going places."

Surprised, I ask, "Have you that much control without a motor?"

With a touch of the lecturer, Carl explains, "There are many forces that create lift. You know, the sun doesn't heat the air. It heats the earth, and the earth in turn heats the air. Heated air rises and creates currents that sweep upward—the currents I ride. Those currents are very substantial, and constantly moving. You know, even if there were no uplift, my plane has a forty-two-foot wingspread, and once I get up I could glide about thirty-eight miles before reaching the ground."

He shakes his head. "But actually, it's never like that. The atmosphere is never still. There are constant updrafts." He considers a moment. "You know, people think of soaring as very peaceful, and I suppose that's part of the pleasure—the stillness, the beauty. Even now there are times when the day draws to an end and I'm cruising back at seven or eight thousand feet when I can relax and enjoy the scenery. Sometimes I'll skirt the edge of a cumulus cloud mass with the red and orange of the sun on it—that's beautiful. But that's not the real pleasure. The real pleasure is the sense of accomplishment it gives me."

"You mean the accomplishment of staying up?"

"Sure, staying up is a battle itself. But what I'm getting at is that soaring itself isn't a calm and peaceful process. As a matter of fact, it's rarely quiet. There's always the noise of air rushing past the ship. My sailplane is fiberglass and relatively quiet, but there's still noise. You know, you're strapped into that plane without much room to spare and the wings come together just behind you; they almost seem to spring out of your shoulders.

"The canopy is large and in flight the nose is down so your vision is great, but you know, that plane can be thrown about violently. You're always fighting nature, even when you move with her. You can be flying in a safe situation and then, the next second, you're in an air mass that's dropping you right to the ground. The situation changes constantly, and that's what I find intriguing. I'm constantly making decisions."

He hesitates, then paces again. "Sure, I like the feeling that I'm fighting nature every inch of the way, but you know, if it weren't for competitive flying and the challenge of flying a given distance faster than the next guy, of climbing more efficiently, of developing my skills and ability better than anyone else—if it weren't for that, soaring would hold very little pleasure for me."

"Your pleasure is in the challenge?"

"Exactly. And, of course, there's always the element of danger. That gives it spice. When you're flying high, you can be relaxed, but when you're low you're in imminent danger of making a forced landing. Sometimes I'm filled with apprehension when I'm flying low over a wooded area, desperately searching for some lift. But that apprehension is part of the pleasure.

"You know, most of us who fly sailplanes were once flying powered planes. But powered flying has become so controlled that I can't enjoy it. With soaring, I can go where I please, do what I please, as long as I abide by the regulations."

He turns and looks out the window a moment, then shakes his head as if rejecting the city skyline. "I'll tell you one of the real pleasures of soaring—climbing in waves. It's absolutely still and quiet, like an elevator ride."

"Waves?" I ask.

He nods. "When air passes over high mountains, waves occur on the leeward side and they build up to great altitudes. You can be standing still in relation to the ground, but in effect you're into a headwind and going up in terms of lift, to fifteen, sixteen, even twenty thousand feet—but you seem perfectly still. It's a unique sensation."

He's silent for a moment, then he says, "You know, when you're soaring, sometimes you find yourself circling in a thermal with a hawk. They're the masters of soaring. It's fantastic to fly with them at eight or nine thousand feet and watch them leave the thermal and accelerate as you do—man, that's pleasure!"

"How would a person get into soaring?" I asked.

"Your local airport could probably tell you how to contact the soaring group nearest you. Or the Soaring Society of America, in Los Angeles, could help you out. If the idea appeals to you, by all means check into it. I did—and I love it!"

At Home in the Trees

"When I was in my preteens, eight, nine, and ten, my greatest pleasure was taking a book, an apple, and a hard roll, climbing up in the fork of a tree, and reading for a couple of hours," Chuck tells a group of us. "The apple and roll were for physical sustenance, but the tree—that was sustenance for the soul. Getting up in the branches, propping myself into a comfortable fork—what a feeling! What a sense of self-sufficiency! I was alone, safe, secure —nothing could get at me up there. In the first place, no one was likely to look up and notice me. And even if they did, I was too far away for them to bother me. That tree would become my special place, my very private place. Even if I didn't read, if I just sat there and munched apples, or climbed simply to be alone, it was still a wonderful and magical place."

"But weren't you a city boy?" I ask.

"Oh, sure," said Chuck, "but there was a big park that bordered the river, and I'd find my climbing trees there. Maybe that was what made it so special. I had to go a long way to find a tree to climb."

"That's a funny thing," Tony says. "I was a city boy too, and there just weren't any trees big enough to climb in our part of town. But we had something almost as good. We had billboards."

"Billboards?" We all look at him in surprise, and he explains.

"Sure, you know, half the empty lots had billboards on them, and the bracing behind the billboards was an intricate mass of boards, like struts—or like a jungle gym, that park toy. We'd get some scrap lumber from the building sites and climb up the struts and build a platform about fifty feet or so above the ground. We'd have a little spot there that was private and secret. The younger kids couldn't get to us because it took some skill to climb the framework behind the billboards. But we older kids, we'd swing up easily whenever we wanted to. It was great, a lot like Chuck's forked tree. We had the same quiet and privacy, and no adult could reach us. That was important."

Sylvia, listening to Chuck and Tony, smiles. "I was a country girl—or at least suburban. We had a house about twenty miles from the city. There was a lawn all around it, but about a quarter of a mile in back there was a heavy stand of maples, big gnarled and knotted trees. My father and my two older brothers built me a tree house in one of the maples when I was ten years old."

She sighs. "You know, even now, when I go home for a visit, I manage to sneak away and climb up to the tree house. The roof and floor are still solid. Actually, it's built in two trees that are close together. The floor is laid on two big beams nailed to both trees. The walls had window and door openings, but now they've rotted away.

"It's a heavenly spot. It's always cool up there because the leaves shade the roof and reflect the sunlight. I can sit there, dangling my legs, and if I close my eyes my entire childhood comes back. Sometimes I could just cry, it's so bittersweet!"

"That's great if you want to recapture your childhood," Tony says. "For my part, all I want is to forget it. I'm thoroughly convinced, thank God, that you can't go back again."

"Not for real," Chuck says quickly, "but in memory you certainly can. Even now, if I come on the right kind of tree and swing myself up into one of the branches, I get the same feeling that Sylvia does in her tree house. I just close my eyes, and I can taste the hard rolls and apples!"

"Maybe a grown man can't go around climbing billboards," Tony laughs. "But I can certainly remember the joy I used to get out of it."

Listening to them, I interrupt to ask, "Is all the pleasure of it in memory only? Is it just a childhood pleasure? I know I've built tree houses for my children and they've loved them, but what about someone our age?"

"I know I still enjoy my tree house," Sylvia says. "Part of it is nostalgia, sure, but a lot of it is that same old sense of being somewhere no one else can get to, in a fortress all your own."

Slightly embarrassed, Tony confesses, "I climb trees, even now—when I can get away from everyone else. I'm too old for billboards, but last summer I was out hiking in the Catskills and I found a big, branched tree near the top of Slide Mountain. You know, I climbed up, telling myself it was just to get a view above the trail, but once there I just settled down and stayed for half an hour. A group of hikers passed below, and I didn't say anything, just tucked myself quietly into the tree and watched them. Sure, the pleasure comes from the memory of childhood, and nostalgia, but it's also in just being up there, above the ground, in your own private little world."

# Free Body, Free Spirit

I have lunch with Chuck in a health-food store, and afterward we walk to the park and sit on a bench while Chuck talks about the pleasures of yoga.

"There are many kinds of yoga," he explains, "and they involve different levels of awareness. Essentially, as I practice it, yoga is a freeing exercise. It breaks down physical tension to free my body, and, supposedly, with my body, my spirit."

Chuck is tall and lean. His eyes, a pale green, seem to glow with a peculiar intensity. I find it uncomfortable to meet his eyes. Detecting a note of doubt in his "supposedly," I ask how fully he goes along with the freeing concept.

"It works for me. I know where I'm at."

"And in terms of pleasure?"

"Well, my whole being has become a source of pleasure since I've gotten into yoga. I'm able to experience so much more joy in every waking hour."

"How long have you been into it?"

"Over two years. I was an unhappy dancer for years, frustrated because of my own insecurities and fears. I wasn't able to really enjoy dancing because of the things going on inside my head. Now it's different. I'm not trying to get anywhere professionally in dance. I do it for my own pleasure. But I know my pleasure in dance has really come from yoga. I owe it to my instructor, who's taught me how yoga can be a centering experience."

"What do you mean, centering?"

"It means working from within, using the whole process of exercise and meditation. The energy I desire can be gotten through deep meditation—and as my energy expands, my perception expands. I open each tension area in my body. I breathe easier and I enjoy life more. I become aware of the pleasure of living on a twenty-four-hour basis."

"But how much of this is yoga?"

"All of it. You see, people in our society are bound up, desensitized, conditioned so we're not aware of our own craziness.

"Yoga integrates awareness into breathing. It allows you to relate to everything you come in contact with." Chuck stretches his arms to include the park, the paths, the trees and rocks. "It's a way of getting out of your head by becoming aware of the energy all around you—in rocks as well as people."

"You mean energy is the same as matter?"

"Yes. It doesn't ever stop. You can relate to anything and draw energy out of it. I once picked up an antique ring with a bloody history, and a shock went through my body as the energy that ring had picked up in all its years went through me. I was aware of that energy and able to respond to it because of my yoga."

"Is that part of the pleasure of yoga?"

"To me, yes. Yoga has taught me a freedom in the act of breathing. A lot of the veils over my eyes that allowed me to do head trips are gone. Now the sensation of my body comes through and that's pleasure. It's a heightening of my perceptions, my awareness, my total act of living!

"Even the sports I go in for—swimming, running—they're all easier. I have better control of my muscles as well as my spirit."

"But is yoga just an exercise?"

"It's basically an exercise in breathing, but it's much more.

You're taught to pull in your breath through the hole in the bridge of your nose—"

"Your nostrils?" I ask, confused.

"No. The bridge of your nose. Imagine a hole there. You can feel the warmth gather in your chest, your heart. You focus deep inside to expand your energies. Your lungs are used very little. You breathe with your diaphragm. You learn to let go and surrender, let the energy flow from point to point in your body.

"After four or five sessions you can feel your body vibrate in waves, from the tip of your spine, as tensions are unblocked."

Dubiously I ask, "All this from a way of breathing?"

"And much more. How you use yoga depends on yourself, your power of concentration, your developing sense of awareness." Chuck leans back and looks up at the sky. "At this point in my development I'm able to feel pleasure constantly. Other people's craziness doesn't bother me. I breathe and rise above them. Eventually I hope to be my own man completely, responsible for myself for good or bad."

He straightens up, closes his eyes, and takes a deep breath, his face peaceful. "I still haven't made it. I'm still afraid to risk rejection or failure, but I'm learning. Now I know that unless I take risks I can't prove myself. I know it in my mind, but the next step is to know it with my body—and yoga is guiding me toward that."

The Silence
and the Surface

"I remember a day skiing at Aspen, the last day of my week there, as a matter of fact," Jim says. "Everyone was warning me about the last run of the day, but I couldn't resist. I went up and looked down the twelve-thousand-foot slope, and, would you believe it, it was empty! I had hurt my left leg earlier, and now, as I started down, I found that I was favoring it. Partway down I fell, and when I picked myself up and started down again, I found that I had tightened up. I started talking to myself as I went, 'You can make it ... now do this ... this way ... take it easy here ... you're doing swell ,,, attaboy ...' By the time I reached the bottom I was shouting."

"It sounds scary."

"No, it wasn't at all. It was a wonderful feeling of exhilaration. You know, that's what I love about skiing—that exhilaration, that sense of freedom. I get a fantastic pleasure out of the grace of that sweeping descent down a snowy face!" He smiles as he recalls it. "And that view down the mountain."

Jim is in his fifties, lean and active and filled with a nervous kind of energy. "All the bother, the travel and preparation, the expense and the hassle—they're all worth that trip down. How can I describe it to you?"

"I don't ski, so you'll have to."

"Well, first there's the quiet. There's no noise except the sound of your skis. Then there's the speed, and a sense of grace if you're doing it right. You feel proud in your technique . . ." He hesitates, thoughtful. "I think a great deal of the pleasure is mixed up with pride, simple pride at your own achievement."

"And the danger?" I ask.

"Oh, yes, there's always an element of danger. The danger is linked to speed, and you can't really get the fullest pleasure out of skiing unless you go fast enough to be at the edge of danger. I think of it as controlled disaster. The smallest error and you're wiped out. You can break an ankle, a leg, or a knee.

"You know, in the beginning you're usually afraid. I remember being on top of a mountain with a friend. The slope was covered with powder—that's fresh snow—and it was dangerous, but we both felt we had to go down. In the beginning our skis were almost trapped by the snow, but partway down we suddenly got the rhythm. At that point the fear left me. Instead I had a tremendous feeling of exhilaration—and achievement. The rest of the descent went faster. I was more confident and more graceful."

"Then the pleasure is in the movement?"

"In a way, yes, and in the sense of speed. You can't really enjoy yourself when you're skiing slowly."

"Is it the same thrill you get out of a speeding car?"

"No, not really. In a car you're removed from the road by the body of the car. When you ski you're in more intimate contact with the surface, but aside from the speed, there's the pleasure you get out of a thing well done. You know, it's a little like dancing. You use your entire body. When you're going very fast, you'll often huddle into a racing tuck, and you'll check occasionally, changing your weight and angling the skis—it's all tremendously exciting.

"There's another thing, and it's linked to the danger element.

It happens when you're going fast and you hit a patch of ice. For a moment, then, you're out of control. That moment is wild. You realize the danger and your stomach drops, but the feeling is a mixture of, well, pleasure and pain, ecstasy and fear, blended together. It's so intense!

"At other times there can be a total abandonment, like when you come down in the 'milking-stool' position, relaxing and putting all your weight back from your knees—or there's the pleasure of just skiing automatically, without thinking or concentrating on the how of it, just abandoning yourself to the immediate sensation.

"And, of course, when it's over, at the end of a day's skiing, there's such a catharsis, such a sense of accomplishment—everything seems better, the food, the fire at the lodge, reliving the day with the other skiers. You know, there's a great deal of companionship on the lift, waiting in line, at night in the lodge—and yet skiing itself is a solitary sport. In the final analysis you're out there by yourself. You look down the mountain and you get that awful feeling of unease—am I going down that . . . alone!"

Jim is a downhill skier, but when I talk to Sarah, who does cross-country skiing, she tells me, "Speed isn't involved. You go through the woods, poling your way along, and sure, you're going faster than if you walked, but you're less involved with how you're doing it than where you're doing it. There's a silence to the woods when there's a deep snow over everything, and a sense of beauty, a serenity. Everything is clean and sparkling. The brooks are silent, or if they run they're down deep, under the ice. The trees are all bare, except the evergreens, and it's all hushed and reverent. You're high off the ground, sometimes a foot or more above it, and the underbrush doesn't bother you. It's all covered with snow, and you glide along on top of it as if you were suspended in the air!

"It's a feeling of"—she frowns, trying to find the right words —"of belonging. You're not alien to the woods. You're part of them. That's what brings me the greatest pleasure."

My Job Works for Me

"What I object to," Murray says, "is people who tell me I should have a good time, relax, and do things. They say, Come home early and take it easy. Play a little golf. Get a hobby. Read—don't they understand that I enjoy my work? That's what really gives me pleasure."

"But there's more to life than work." Hearing how inane this sounds, I add, "Doesn't one make the other better?"

"Well, look, I have a wife and kids. I love my wife and the boys too, but am I an unnatural father because I don't get a great kick out of spending time with them? I spend some time because I think it's good for them, but I don't do it for my own pleasure."

We order our lunch and Murray butters a roll. He points the knife at me accusingly. "I think most fathers kid themselves when they say they enjoy playing with their kids. Mine are five and seven. What can kids that age offer a grown man?"

Thoughtfully he adds, "I've always been work-oriented. I was a businessman when I was still a kid. I never really enjoyed the games the other kids played. My family didn't need the money, but I got a kick out of delivering orders for the local stores. I used to hustle up and down the whole neighborhood.

"When I was in high school I organized a messenger service one summer. I hired kids my own age to deliver messages and wound up with my own service, called it the Educated Messenger Service. It didn't last because I had to go back to school, but I tell you, I had more fun that summer than I had in a long time. I got a tremendous sense of satisfaction out of organizing and running the business. I get the same thing out of business now."

Our lunch comes and we eat quietly for a while, then I ask, "What is the pleasure? Is it accomplishment?"

"Partly, partly." He considers. "A lot of it is like a puzzle. You know how good you feel when you finish a puzzle and everything fits together? Well, I get that same sense of accomplishment when I put over a business deal and everything works out perfectly.

"I kid myself sometimes by pretending that I work hard for my family, to give them the things they want, but that's self-deception. Hell, my wife likes the good life, but she'd be happy without it."

"Would she rather have more of you?"

"Now that's a funny thing. She has as much of me as I can give, and she realizes that. We've made peace with each other over the years. She has a life of her own—the kids, the home, the neighbors, her organizations—and she's content in it." Ruefully he adds, "I'm sort of a status symbol in that life, the husband who makes it all socially acceptable, and I go to all her social events as just that, the husband on display.

"But my real life, the life I enjoy and get the greatest pleasure out of, is my life at the office. That's where the challenges are—and the accomplishment. In a sense, that's reality and my life at home is a fantasy."

"Then why have a wife and children?"

"A good question." He considers his empty plate, then says,

"To be honest, I guess I use my family as my wife uses me—an excuse to indulge my pleasure. Her pleasure is the home, and I'm her excuse to keep it. My pleasure is the job, and she's my excuse for working so hard."

"And the Protestant ethic?"

"No, no. It's not that at all. You see, I enjoy the work. It's no sacrifice, no imposition. I don't work hard because of guilt. I work hard simply because I like my job—it works for me, I don't work for it! I see every work problem as a fascinating challenge, and I react like a chess player. Maybe playing chess is hard work, but it's also fun. My business deals are hard work, but fun too. I enjoy manipulating people, seeing elaborate preparations pay off.

"I'm at my best when I work my hardest. I sleep well and I eat well. Let me go off on a vacation, and suddenly I can't sleep through the night. I'm uneasy and restless. We recently bought a summer place where my wife and kids go as soon as school is out. I join them on weekends. That works out best of all. I give lip service to a vacation, but I can still do my job." He grins. "It sounds crazy, I'll admit, but when all is said and done, my real pleasure is in work."

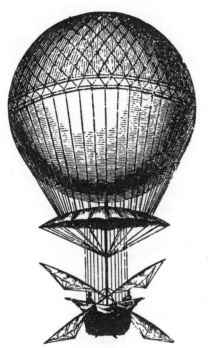

Inside the Wind

When I think of ballooning, I always think of *The Wizard of Oz* and that frustrating scene when the great balloon soars off with the Wizard while Dorothy holds Toto in her arms and yells, "Come back for me!"

I tell this to Jerry, the balloonist, and he laughs.

"There's actually no reason why the Wizard couldn't have come back," he tells me. "It would have been the easiest thing in the world for him to lower his balloon and hover while Dorothy scrambled in. We balloonists play a game where we attach tacks to the bottom of the gondola and fill a little rubber balloon with air, then attach an egg to it. The point is to lower the big balloon gently enough so that the tacks pop the little balloon without breaking the egg."

Puzzled, I say, "I always thought of a balloon as an unwieldy, clumsy monster, pulling at its ropes in an effort to tear free."

"It isn't like that at all," Jerry says. "The balloon I fly is made of rip-stop nylon and the gondola, or basket, is wicker, sturdy and big enough to sit in comfortably, and there's the burner and gas cylinders."

"Gas?"

"Yes, to fuel the burners. The burners are attached to a ring under the open mouth of the balloon. The burner heats the air in the balloon and, since hot air rises, the balloon lifts up." Jerry, a tall, lean man in his late thirties, with intense blue eyes, frowns as he tries to explain. "A balloon wants to fly, to float, and, well, become a part of nature. If you try to rope it and hold it down, you don't get the real sensation of floating with the wind. Those balloons at fairs with ropes holding them—they're not at all like free balloons."

Smiling, he says, "The first time I soloed, it was 7 A.M. That's when the air is cool and most quiet. I saw three deer feeding below me, and I came down to within fifty feet of them. They just stood and looked up at me, then went back to their feeding. I didn't bother them at all until I had to turn on my burners for some lift. Then the noise startled them and they leaped away.

"I was so excited on that flight—I came down low enough to pick leaves off the trees—in fact, I lodged in the top of a tree until I turned on my burner and lifted."

"You like floating low?"

"Yes. It's a special pleasure. I've floated over water where people were in boats. One man in a motorboat offered me coffee. A wind came up and I couldn't quite reach him, but he caught up to me with his boat and I finally got the drink."

He pauses a moment. "There's a sense of camaraderie when you're in a balloon. You meet people easily. About three weeks ago we took off from a golf course, and landed in eight different farms! At each one we kept the balloon inflated. The farmers and their families all came out to say hello and bring us food. Sometimes we'd take them for a little ride—most people haven't seen balloons before and it's an exciting experience to them. It's funny, I've never met anyone that way who was hostile. Everyone is friendly, and you meet some fascinating people, professors, lawyers, secretaries—"

"Is that what you like best about it?"

"No—I like that, but chiefly it's the sense of freedom, of getting away from all your troubles, soaring free. It's like"—he bites his lip a moment—"well, imagine waking up and finding yourself floating above the earth. Things on the ground look very small, like toys. I think one of the great things about a balloon is flying close enough to the ground to see everything. And the silence! An airplane is all noise and speed, but a balloon—well, there is no sound of wind, no matter how hard it blows. You see, you're inside the wind!"

"Inside the wind?"

"Yes. What I mean is that there's no relative wind. You're moving with it at its speed, so there's no feeling of movement. You hang motionless—the gas burner doesn't flicker even though you might be in a twenty-mile-per-hour wind. You're a part of that wind, see?

"People have a strange idea that balloons are shaky. They're not, and they're safe. You could shoot a cannonball through the nylon and the hole wouldn't matter. You'd just turn up the burners a bit. It's not like a toy balloon, which is a bag under pressure. See?"

I nod, and he continues. "Also, no matter how gray it is outside when you start, you can go right up in a balloon and you're in blue sky and sunshine. I remember being six thousand feet over Iowa on a hot summer day and it was ten to fifteen degrees cooler.

"What I really love about it is the solitude, the sense of freedom, of looking down on the world, but not rushing past it. When you ascend it's like being drawn up into the sky, like a rocket rises, but in slow, slow motion.

"You can hear people, too. I think you hear differently when you're up above like that. You pass over streams and you can hear water tumbling over the rocks, echoes, dogs barking, all at fifty to a hundred feet, and then you lift up to five hundred or a thousand and all is silence.

"The thing is, you have an infinity of altitudes to choose, from a few feet to thousands. I've landed on mountaintops that would take two days to climb, deflated the balloon, slept overnight, and the next day reinflated and taken off. And you're not helpless.

There's always a wind in one direction or another. At one altitude the wind can be going one way, and a thousand feet higher it can be blowing in another direction. You learn to maneuver up and down to ride the different winds."

"Is it frightening?"

He shrugs. "Oh, I was very frightened the first time I went up, but in a few minutes the fear left me. You go up so easily, you really can't stay frightened.

"You know, you have to take off when the wind is under seven miles an hour—early in the morning or late in the afternoon—and any rain but a very light shower will keep you grounded. Rain cools the balloon too quickly. So the conditions must be perfect for take-off, and maybe that allays the fear. And anyway, the sense of floating is worth a little fear—in the beginning. It never stays with you for long once the excitement fills you."

"How would I get started if I wanted to try ballooning?"

"There are ballooning clubs all over America—the Balloon Federation of America has its headquarters in Washington, D.C., and there's a group called the Balloon Platoon based in Bloomfield Hills, Minnesota. Your local phone book would probably tell you if there's a branch in your area. Believe me, it's worth trying to get inside the wind."

Patterns of Pleasure

Florence smooths out a white cotton shirt with a geometric design in black and red cross-stitch, exquisitely intricate.

"I'm into ethnic embroidery now," she says. "This is Czechoslovakian. Last year I took a tour of the Soviet Union, and I wasn't interested in any of the usual tourist sights. Instead I'd follow women on the street just to see the type of embroidery on their clothes. You can pinpoint exact geographical regions by embroidery style."

"And you really enjoy it?"

"Enjoy it? If I had my way I'd do nothing but sit home all day and embroider, or do needlepoint or bargello—it gives me a sense of precision, of knowing exactly what I'm going to do next."

Laughing, Florence pushes back her dark, disordered hair. "I need this sense of order in my life. The kids, the house, and my job are so chaotic. In my needlepoint there's discipline. It's like"—

searching for the right words, she takes a few tentative stitches—
"my needlework is a control against the anarchy all around me.

"For instance, a needlepoint problem always has an answer, so
I can be more disciplined with it than with anything else. If I make
a mistake, discover a stitch out of line, I'll think nothing of ripping
out six inches to correct it. You can't do that with life. Here I do a
piece and I finish it, I have a sense of completion."

"Do you enjoy the creative part of needlepoint?"

"Creative?" She shakes her head. "It may be creative for some
people, but I'm just not a creative person. I couldn't, for the life of
me, come up with an original design, and I don't really want to.
There's no original thinking involved in what I do, that's part of
my pleasure. I love to copy. I follow directions, sometimes extremely complicated directions. When I follow them perfectly, I
feel wonderfully fulfilled."

She looks down at her work with a touch of surprise. "I never
thought it out before, but what I really like is the feeling of
precision, of giving my best interpretation to what someone else
has stated."

She embroiders a few lines, then puts her needle down. "In
school I always benefited from the mistakes the other kids made.
That's what this is like."

"I'm not sure I understand."

"Well, someone else has gone through all the errors, and he's
put down a perfect pattern. I follow that pattern and I benefit from
all the errors he's made to get it."

"I see. Do you give your sewing away when you finish it?"

"Never!" She sits up straight. "I can't bear to part with any of
it. Every piece is too much a part of me. It's such a personal thing."
She smooths out the embroidery again. "It's all mine."

"Do you get more pleasure out of the harder patterns?"

"Yes. The harder it is, the more satisfaction it gives me. People
admire it, and I realize that I've made a thing of beauty. It's kind of
a status thing with me. The harder the project, the more respect I
get, because none of my friends can do such intricate work."

"Does embroidery give you any other pleasure?"

"Oh, certainly. The very act of embroidering or doing needlepoint relaxes me and reduces my tension. The work becomes a

haven for me. I can take it out at any time in any situation and get rid of my annoyances or my boredom.

"Then there's the Protestant ethic." She smiles. "I must have 'busy hands' or I'm wasting time."

She hesitates. "There's another pleasure too. Doing this work leaves me free to fantasize, to exercise my mind, to think of dozens of other things. I can't watch TV and do needlepoint, but I can do needlepoint and let my mind roam. Some of my most creative thinking has come while I'm embroidering.

"You see, to me needlepoint is a refuge, but I only allow myself to do it when all of my household chores are finished. Otherwise I think I'd become an addict. Some people are, you know."

She laughs. "It may not be so terrible to be addicted, but I think, at that point, the pleasure would go out of it."

Physical Chess

Fred takes off his mask and guard and replaces his foil, then joins me at the side of the room.

"That was a good workout," he says. "I could use a shower."

"I can wait while you take one."

"No. I'd rather dry out first. Wow!" He takes a deep breath. "I should fence more often."

"You enjoy it."

"Oh, yes. What I enjoy most about it is the one-to-one element, the idea of battling an adversary. You know, fencing is really an unusual sport."

"In what way?"

"You need tremendous coordination, speed, and ability—but, more important, you have to be able to understand your opponent psychologically."

"Why psychologically?"

"You have to figure out what he's going to do before he does it.

It's like chess with the physical element added. You anticipate your opponent's move, counteract it, then make your own move to attack—it's defense and offense, just as in chess."

"Is the pleasure all in the battle?"

"Well—there's pleasure in the act of holding a sword. The sword becomes a part of you, an extension that makes you bigger than you are. But to me the greatest part is the coordinated act of using my head and body together. It adds a certain tension to the conflict."

"But doesn't the tension make you anxious?"

"Yes," he says, "but you see, even that anxiety is pleasant. It isn't strong enough to worry me, just intense enough to make me operate more carefully. You know, the best way I can describe the pleasure of fencing—if you're good at it—is to say there's a feeling of preparation, like when you walk into an exam knowing the answers, or when you sit in on a poker game and draw a great hand. I guess I'm trying to say that I enjoy the mastery of the situation."

Leaning back against the wall, he adds, "You don't get that sense of mastery in many sports. It's a kind of total awareness of mind and body, of every aspect of yourself, and also of every move of your opponent. I can't think of any other activity that gives you that same feeling in that same way."

"What about boxing?" I ask.

"Yes," he says, "but there's a lot of pain in boxing. Here there's no pain. Your real pleasure in fencing comes when your body is under complete control. You're in perfect balance, and you move as if you're dancing. To the joys of movement, balance, and grace you add the pleasure of competition.

"You know, we all have aggressive impulses that we have to control in order to get along with other people. Maybe most sports are opportunities to get rid of those impulses. From that point of view, fencing is a perfect outlet. You can get rid of your hostility without the danger of hurting anyone."

"Yet swordplay was originally designed to hurt."

"But fencing isn't swordplay. Fencing is a symbolic and styl- ized game. Every thrust or riposte has a counterstroke, but the foil is too flexible to do any harm. It's all part of a pattern, but the speed, the skill, the anticipation of your opponent's move—all these determine the winner, not the hurt you inflict."

He smiles. "You know, I still remember the pleasure of my college dueling bouts, especially the last one, even though I don't remember whether our school won or lost. What I remember is the tension and excitement of the game and the pleasure of working out for hours to get into shape.

"Working out with foils becomes almost mindless after a while. You try to react automatically, but there's such a soothing quality to the drill you go through, such a sense of achievement in getting it just right, that there are times when you'll work out until you literally drop of exhaustion. You become completely caught up in the rhythm of the thing and you forget yourself. It's the most pleasant pleasure I know!"

The Sensuous Feline

I sit down with Judy in her living room, and I find my eyes level
with a cat on a chest of drawers a few feet away. It's a white cat
with pale-green eyes and it stares at me and through me with
infinite disdain. At the same time a calico clown of a cat rubs
against my legs mewing plaintively.

Judy sits down smiling and a third cat, a tortoise-shell, lands in
her lap. She strokes it absently as she talks to me.

"The most wonderful thing about cats," she says, "is their
fur."

I had expected all sorts of things, but not this. "Really? Their
fur?"

"Sure. They're very warm and cuddly, you know." She rubs
the tortoise-shell's belly. "Most people think all cats are stand-
offish, like Sam up there." She nods at the white cat, who flicks a
disdainful glance at her. "Sam is strictly a don't-touch-me type,
but Max here can't get enough petting. He'll snuggle up and bite

you and kiss you and pull your hair—he'll be all over you with that delicious soft fur."

The calico cat is still rubbing my leg. I pick him up and put him on my lap, stroking him tentatively while Judy smiles encouragement. "Oscar there is the same way. Show him some affection and he can't get enough.

"You know, most people don't realize that cats are as loving as dogs. They just aren't as servile. Dogs will go to any extreme to please you, but not cats. They have a tremendous amount of self-respect and dignity." She hesitates. "They also have an uncanny consciousness of what's happening."

"How do you mean?"

"Well, it's hard to explain, but they seem to sense and reflect your own moods. They're also aware of their own presence. They seem to look at themselves and see their own actions." As I continue to look puzzled, she goes on, "Now take dogs. A dog is embarrassed if he does something awkward or silly, but a cat is self-conscious all the time. Cats have such elaborate rituals of behavior and play. You know, a cat will play with you as long as you play its game, but try to take over and it loses interest."

"Do they have their own games?"

"Oh, yes. Hide-and-go-seek, teasing each other, playing with balls and strings and toys—they love to play, and I get great pleasure out of watching them. They have this idea that they should be graceful, and they hurt their pride when they do something klutzy—or, I should say, some do. That's the thing about cats. They're all different.

"Oscar, there, is a great player. He'll play all the time, with a ball, with string—any game he can get into. Max just wants to be held and cuddled. He's basically a lover, and he'll go to any extent to be petted. Sam just wants to pose and be admired. He's always immaculate, always with his front paws together and his head lifted, just so. Some cats spend their whole life fighting, day and night—it's the variety of cat personalities that gets me."

"What's your chief feeling about them?"

"I guess it's a sensual one. I love their tremendous variety of furs, the long, fluffy coats and the short, smooth coats, Each feels differently and each is beautiful. Just sitting and watching them move, watching the way the fur ripples, gives me so much pleasure. Sam poses, and I appreciate his pose. Sometimes I'll spend almost an hour just staring at him, or watching Oscar play."

She pauses a moment, chewing her lip. "I think there's something of a love-hate relationship with cats. In some corner of ourselves we seem basically afraid of them. They appear to know something they aren't telling. It makes some of us self-conscious about the way we act in front of them. I guess it's a hangover from the days of witchcraft, one of those unreasoning fears.

"But when we overcome that uneasiness, we're usually completely captivated by them." She hugs Max to her with sudden fierceness and he reaches up with sheathed claws to stroke her. "You've heard the expression 'the cat's whiskers.' Well, their whiskers are a real turn-on. All this soft fur, and then as the cat snuggles in you feel those harsh whiskers—it's a terrific contrast.

"Watching a mother cat with her kittens is another pleasure, the way she teaches them and cleans them. As for the kittens themselves—well, they're something else again. They're sweet and charming, but they don't turn me on the way grown cats do. Kittens are all the same. But cats! Every one is a different pleasure."

Loafing Around

I join Larry at the counter of our summer cabin and watch him measure out a tablespoon of butter, a tablespoon of sugar, a cup of milk, and precise quantities of salt, molasses, yeast, white flour, and whole-wheat flour. He arranges all the ingredients neatly in a row on the counter. His last words, as our wives drove into town to shop, were, "Don't get bread. I'll bake."

"Do you really enjoy baking?" I ask him.

"Tremendously." He scalds the milk, then adds the butter, sugar, molasses and salt, sprinkles in two packets of dried yeast, and mixes the liquid into the flour. It's all done carefully, with a sense of ritual.

"But what's the fun in it?" I ask.

"It's many things," Larry says as he mixes the dough, a loose, soggy mess that gradually thickens till he can lift it out of the bowl and put it on the floured counter. "Time me, will you?" he asks as he begins to knead. "Ten minutes should do it."

I watch him as he gets into a rhythm, kneading slowly at first, then moving faster and more competently. He comes down on the mass of dough with the heel of his hand, bends and folds it, flips it a quarter turn, then comes down again, around and around until gradually the dough becomes smoother, more even and satiny.

"This gives it texture," he explains. "It does away with air bubbles. Do you want to try it?"

I back away, shaking my head. "It looks too easy. I can tell it's something I'd mess up in three minutes."

"It is hard to get the knack," Larry admits, laughing. "That's part of the fun of baking, the fact that there are skills to it and you have to learn them to do it well. But aside from that, there's something very soothing, very comfortable about the act of kneading. Once you get into the rhythm of it, it eases away your tensions. Ten or fifteen minutes of kneading is equal to one Valium! That's a real part of the pleasure of baking."

"And the rest of the pleasure?"

"I think there's a big sense of accomplishment. I'm doing something very important, very basic to life. Sure, you can go into any supermarket and pick up a loaf of bread, but this is different. It tastes better and I know it's pure. I know the ingredients I use are perfect, but, more than that, there's a real joy in having made it myself.

"Madge loves my bread—or at least she tells me she does—and the kids get a big kick out of 'Daddy's baking,' so I'm doing something for my family, something down-to-earth. I get their admiration and approval. Whenever they taste bread, they compare it to mine. 'You call this bread? My dad makes a bread. . . .' Now maybe it's silly, but the pleasure I get out of that is tremendous."

Later, when the dough has risen, Larry punches it back, re-kneads it, and divides it into loaves. "And I get pleasure out of the actual act of baking, the variations I add to standard recipes, even finding old-fashioned recipes and following them. In a way, it's all creative."

That evening, when the smell of fresh-baked bread fills the cabin, I find my mouth watering. Larry looks at me and smiles. "I'm getting pleasure out of your face right now! And wait till you taste it. Then you can share my pleasure."

Madge serves it at dinner, still warm and cut into generous slices. I take some and perhaps it's no better than any home-baked bread, but somehow I enjoy it more than I've enjoyed bread in a long time.

And looking at Larry's proud face I begin to understand the pleasures of baking bread.

Idol Pastimes

Lisa's thirteen-year-old niece is a rock freak.

"I don't understand the girl," Lisa tells me. "She gets hysterical over Alice Cooper—my God! Alice Cooper! And her other hero is Mick Jagger—ech."

Lisa's mother smiles and says, "Let's see, it was how many years ago—nine or ten?—that you were screaming at the Beatles."

"Oh, Mother!" Lisa looks at her in mock despair. "It's not the same, I was only thirteen—" She pauses a moment, then laughs. "Well, maybe it was similar."

Curiously I ask, "What pleasure did you get out of the Beatles?"

Reflectively, Lisa says, "In a way it was a sexual thing, but before I knew anything about men at all. It was a kind of initiation into sex, but it was—well, safe."

"Safe?" I ask.

"I didn't know the Beatles, and I couldn't possibly be involved with them. They never demanded anything of me, and then too, they were all handsome and acceptable."

"I'd hardly call Ringo handsome."

"Well, the others were, and even Ringo had an attraction, but, most important, my friends all loved them too. There was what the psychologists call 'peer group acceptance.'"

She shakes her head. "You know, they were the first men I could love outside of my own family. I even got pleasure out of screaming when I saw them."

"Pleasure?"

"Yes. It was a release of sexual energy before I was really able to feel sex—or, rather, to understand my feelings about sex."

She smiles at her mother. "Also, the most important part of it all was that our parents didn't like them one bit. We could have them all to ourselves, and with all our screaming and carrying on we could rebel against our parents."

Lisa's mother nods. "I can understand it perfectly."

Surprised, Lisa asks, "How?"

"Well, I went through the same pleasure with Frank Sinatra when I was a teen-ager. It was a very sexual feeling."

"What was there about him that turned you on?" I ask.

"Well—" She frowns, remembering. "It's funny, but I think it was his phrasing, more than anything else, the way he used words. It seemed as if his songs had an explicit sexual meaning just for me."

"Mom!" Lisa says, half amused, half shocked.

"Well, odd as it seems, we could feel sex too—and that terribly intense hero worship. Benny Goodman and his band played in our town back in the late thirties, and I sneaked down to see him and he shook my hand. Would you believe it, I didn't wash that hand for two weeks! The pleasure was sexual, sure, but it was also hero worship—maybe that's always sexual."

"I don't think so," Paul, Lisa's English boy friend, breaks in. "I was a Beatlemaniac too when I was fourteen or so. But it was mainly McCartney I worshiped and wanted to be like—I even played a guitar. The glamour and the adulation he received gave me pleasure. Hero worship let me be part of the scene. I saved clippings about them, and when I was thirteen I went to see *A Hard Day's Night*. Everyone was screaming, the guys as well as the girls, so I pitched in and screamed too."

"Did you enjoy it?"

"Well, you know, it was the thing to do, and then it was newsmaking. The Beatle followers were also photographed for the telly, and what pleasure to see yourself on the screen!

"And, of course, there was the actual pleasure of listening to their music, you know. Over the years it kept getting better and better. I was basking in reflected glory."

"They were so charmingly irreverent," Lisa says.

"Of course," says Paul. "They were always questioning the establishment, and that allowed us to question the establishment too. When they did something outrageous, like telling off an adult, we felt it was youth conquering age."

"When I was young . . ." I hesitated. Who were the teen-age idols then? Lindbergh? Babe Ruth? Joe Louis? Did any of them tell off the establishment? And yet I could readily recall the pleasures of identification, of collecting pictures of my heroes, reliving their adventures. The pleasure, I realize, lies in identification, in the vicarious living of another more successful, more exciting life.

"But Alice Cooper . . ." Lisa says sadly, and we're all quiet for a moment.

Past Perfect

We're rummaging through a thrift shop and Melissa finds a tattered organdy dress from the thirties, miraculously still in one piece. She holds it up in front of her and smiles dreamily.

"Should I get it?" she asks. "It's only a dollar, and look, it's just like the one Ginger Rogers wore in *Swingtime*."

"Where would you wear it?" I ask.

Melissa looks at me in surprise. "Wear it? I just want to have it. It doesn't fit me anyway."

Later I ask her, "What is the fun of nostalgia? I know you love to watch old movies, but what pleasure do you get out of them?"

She thinks a moment and tries to explain. "I guess, first of all I go for who's in the movie, say Fred Astaire and Ginger Rogers, or Veronica Lake and Alan Ladd—those are the ones I like best, because they're so predictable."

"But I'd think that would bore you."

"Oh no. You see, they epitomize certain things. They're idealized, not at all real, sort of symbols. Alan Ladd is tough, Clark Gable is masculine, Fred Astaire is suave, and Ginger Rogers is the smart aleck with the heart of gold. None of them is complex or three-dimensional. The women are all beautiful, the men all handsome—it's like a perfect fantasy."

She pauses, frowning. "Look. Your own life may be boring and unpredictable, but when you watch those old movies you get the illusion of control, by identification. You feel you have the potential to be like them. They're showing you how."

Melissa is twenty-two, a bright young woman and a college graduate. I try to understand her fascination with the thirties, a time she never experienced, but I can't quite see it. "Don't the plots sometimes strike you as silly?" I ask her.

"Not really, because I don't for a moment believe any of them. I know they're all fantasy, but they have the charm of a beautiful painting.

"I suppose it's nostalgia for a past I never knew, and one I realize never existed—a simpler, more logical world with a rigid morality. The good guys always win, the bad guys always lose."

"Do you want to go back to that time?"

She laughs. "How could I? I know that time never was. It's the movie that creates that time. It doesn't represent any real era, it creates a fantasy.

"And the predictability of the fantasy lets you accept the idea that once upon a time morals were different, there was a strict code of behavior that everyone followed, and the double standard was always accepted."

Surprised, I remind Melissa that she's always opposed the double standard. "I thought you were for women's rights!"

"Of course," she says impatiently, "but that's what I want in the *real* world. We're talking about a fantasy world, a world where the double standard was beneficial to both sexes. That's important. Chivalry worked because the men were all strong and the women all beautiful. You see, you're a man. What you don't understand is that women, in a way, still feel attracted by the double standard, even if it's wrong. The old movie makers understood that. It's the same pleasure women get out of long dresses and feminine clothes, though we fight for the right to wear pants.

"We can't allow ourselves to follow the old stereotypes in

today's society. We feel a kind of contempt for women who cling to them. They don't understand about liberation."

She hesitates. "There's no law that says a liberated woman is a happier one. Maybe there was pleasure in the old double standard and that's why so many women cling to it—but movies, the old thirties movies, can give us the same pleasure while we fight the standard."

She grins naughtily. "If you're wondering about the pleasures of nostalgia, I might as well confess that when I have time and I'm home in the afternoon, I watch the reruns of the *Mickey Mouse Club.*"

"That I can't understand!" I shake my head in bewilderment.

"But why not? The pleasure is like that of the old movies. It's all clean-cut, simple, with a definite moral code. Orderly and, my God, so predictable. It took place about twenty years ago, and like the old movies it's frozen in time. Some of the actors are old men—others are dead!

"We kids who are afraid of growing old see a kind of immortality there." She becomes serious. "It's the same with the old stars of the thirties. In a sense, it's looking at history. The same is true of the old *Groucho Marx* shows, and *I Love Lucy.*"

Her face lights up. "That's really my favorite, *I Love Lucy.* Corny, predictable, infantile, simplistic, obvious—and I love it. I could watch its reruns for hours."

I shake my head and she laughs. "But that's what nostalgia is all about."

A Walk on the Wild Side

"My idea of absolute pleasure?" Bob smiles. "I get it once a year. Ruth and I land in Zurich and drive four hours through the mountains till we reach Pontresina, near the Italian border in Switzerland. Somehow there's always a navy-blue sky with no clouds. Maybe it's the time of year, my vacation is very rigid—the same time every summer.

"After we settle into a hotel we take the cog railway up the mountain. You know, from the moment the plane lands, I can feel the tensions washing out of me—the personal worries, the anxieties of work—and when I reach the top of that mountain I'm reborn."

"Is that your pleasure?"

"Oh, no, that's when my pleasure begins. Ruth and I hike for two or three hours along the edge of the mountain, through cow pastures, along the sides of cliffs, and at each edge there's a new vista. We see other mountain ranges. I remember one day when the sky was 100 percent clear and blue, and little glider planes were weaving in and out of the mountains."

"Is it the visual beauty that pleases you so?"

"That and more than that. The air is so clear that it just seems to invigorate you. Also, the two of us are completely alone up there, and it's a tough hike. We really have to use our bodies. It's visual and physical, but it's also the contrast between the year I've spent working—and I work hard—and this open, free cleanliness, the panoramas, the constant change in the mountains and being there alone with my wife. You see, by then I'm so sick of other people talking that I could scream."

I smile at that. Bob is a psychiatrist and his working life is tied up with talking people.

"Then," he goes on, "we spend four or five days hiking, getting to know every part of the mountain and the valley where we're staying. After that we take off for our real vacation in Europe."

"That isn't a real vacation?"

"It's more than a vacation. It's a catharsis and a pleasure. Hiking is my greatest pleasure. You see, it involves a simple goal. You go from one place to another, and there's no pressure to worry about anything else, no plans either. You're away from everyone.

"To me the greatest pleasure lies in not having to think about things or figure things out. I'm doing that constantly in my work, looking for answers, uncovering the wheels within the wheels of the mind. My four days of hiking are a total abandonment to a physical and visual experience. But the feeling is not only abandonment *to* something, it's abandonment *of* something—of thinking, worrying, being concerned." He hesitates. "Basically, besides the sense of abandon, I get three things out of hiking; the change in environment, the physical use of my body, and the visual stimulation of what I see."

"Which is most important?"

He shrugs. "It's hard to separate them. Physical exercise in a gym doesn't give me the same pleasure, nor does driving through the country, where the visual stimulus is the same. Come to think of it, there's also the sense of accomplishment when I climb a tough mountain—but that's just an added goodie. It's not essential that I hike up a tough trail to get pleasure out of it. Just walking through an alpine meadow will do it.

"Maybe it's the constant change of scenery. You go through a forest and come out on a meadow and cross it to see a new panorama of mountain and sky. Then, too, part of it has to do with a sense of time. You go at your own speed, no one is driving you, you take as long as you want or go as fast as you want. There are no rules and no restrictions on your enjoyment."

"It's not competitive."

"No. Ruth and I don't compete with each other. In fact, if one of us is tired, the other slows down. I never enjoy hiking with someone who wants to make time or set a record."

"Do you hike in the States?"

"Yes. And of course we have some wonderful hiking here. We've gone off on weekends to state parks and forests and some nearby mountains. We've had some great hikes in the States, but a complete break and an absolutely different environment is even better.

"I guess, in the final analysis, it's a sense of timelessness and a lack of concern for schedules that gives me the greatest pleasure. I have to know I can't be reached, I can't be called back to settle some problem. And one other thing. Out there in the immensity of that alpine beauty no problem seems overwhelming. Everything is put into its proper perspective."

"Is that your idea of what the final analysis will be?"

He looks blank, then laughs at my pun. "When I go to that big couch in the sky, I hope I'll face an open window with an exciting vista of some new alpine valley and mountain. I'll at least get some pleasure out of that!"

Social Gastronomy

I meet Roy at his home to talk about the pleasures of eating out. "Before we start," he says, "I want you to try something new, a real great lager beer. It's called Grolsch, a Dutch brew."

I taste it and nod. "It's good."

"Now that's a pleasure, a new beer you taste for the first time. Like finding a new, good restaurant."

Roy, a dedicated urbanite, takes tremendous pleasure in discovering out-of-the-way little restaurants that serve good food at moderate prices.

"Is it primarily an oral pleasure?" I ask. "I mean, is it the food?"

He shakes his head. "No, I think it's the sense of discovery, of finding a new restaurant very few people know about. There's an excitement to that, especially if the food is good. Well, yes, I guess one of the pleasures is just that, eating really good food."

He hesitates. "It's become a sort of hobby and because of it I've read up on cooking and food in general, studying its history too. I find that the more I know the more sensitive I become to taste the differences, and the more I enjoy the food I eat.

"You know, every national culture has its own food, and there's a tremendous amount of fun in discovering the national food of different groups. This city has a big Puerto Rican population, but it's only recently that I discovered cuchifritos for myself."

"Cuchifritos?"

"Literally, fried pork, all the organ meats from the pig, ears and scraps—they're deep-fried and made into snacks. It's a poverty-type food, but delicious. I get as much fun out of discovering something like that as I do out of eating in a fine French restaurant. It's a different pleasure, but not to be missed."

"Do you favor different ethnic foods?"

"Sure. Today's ethnic food is tomorrow's haute cuisine. When the first Indian restaurants opened in the city I discovered that Indian food is more than just curry sauce to disguise mediocre meat. Their use of yoghurt was fascinating. So was their vegetarian cooking, their breads—and now I've discovered tandori chicken. Wow! That's the 'in' thing now. It's giving Colonel Sanders a run for his money."

"What is it?"

"Chicken cooked on a skewer in a clay oven. You have to taste it to really understand. And then there are the Chinese restaurants. My God, most of America is still in the chow-mein-chop-suey stage, but New York is booming with Szechuan restaurants where they use hot chili to spice up the food. It's really different.

"You know, Chinese food can get very patterned—as a people they love patterned life—but when you break out of the single cooking style, you're in for great pleasure. Originally, most Chinese came here from Canton—in fact, Cantonese was spoken all through Chinatown. Now you hear Mandarin, the people come from Hong Kong or Taiwan, and their styles of cooking are different. Of course, in China there's no such thing as Mandarin cooking. That's a term that originated here, but it describes a fine style of cooking that exists all over China. Cantonese cooking stresses a mixture of ingredients while Szechuan is simple, but hot. Because Taiwan is an island, fish is a heavy staple of its diet.

"I get a great deal of pleasure out of understanding the way food follows immigration. Take Italian food. The original Italian immigrants were mostly southern Italians, and all through the States Italian restaurants—even when the food is good, as it often is—rely heavily on tomato sauce and cheese, like eggplant parmigiana, oily cooking with a good deal of pasta.

"It becomes a rare thing—and so pleasant—when you find an Italian restaurant with the elegant Roman cooking, or with North Italian cooking.

"And all these Japanese restaurants springing up like mushrooms—who ever thought of eating raw fish? Now sushi has taken over and a fine delicate pleasure it is!

"What gives me even more pleasure than the food," he says thoughtfully, "is to see the changing pattern of restaurants in the city—in any big city. This neighborhood, around Twenty-eighth Street, used to be loaded with Armenian restaurants. Then, with the upward mobility of the Armenians, the Indians came in. You can really trace the growth of a city by the growth of its restaurants. I call it social gastronomy. You know," he laughs, "I have a gastronomic theory of history."

"Let me hear it."

"Okay. It goes something like this. After twenty years of hearing China condemned as a threat to world peace—you know, the yellow tide of communism—we see Nixon go over there and our attitude changes overnight. But I believe that we were so quick to accept a new relationship with China because when we think of Chinese food we get a glow of pleasure. If their food is that good, how can the people be bad?"

Smiling, I say, "I don't know how your theory will do in textbooks."

"Well, look at it this way. Have you ever tasted Russian food? It's dull, dreary, colorless—what else can Russia be?"

He throws up his hands. "But Brazilian food! The Brazilians are full of vitality and their food reflects it. The Argentinians are a somber people and not very ingratiating, and neither is their food.

"Seriously, though, like any big city, New York reflects the patterns of immigration through its restaurants. An ethnic group will settle in one area, and you'll get small mom-and-pop restaurants with good food. There are still some old ones left, but new mom-and-pop places aren't springing up much anymore. Small restaurants just aren't making it financially.

"You see, that trend fits my sociological theory—if you stretch it. The decline in restaurant service reflects the decline of the general quality of life. That's the inevitable direction of our civilization. Maybe I should call my theory gastronomic entropy."

"But your pleasures—"

"Ah, that downswing makes the occasional little restaurant with good food and great service and moderate prices all the more pleasant—when I find it. Now just the other day I discovered a Cuban restaurant. Their black beans"—he gestures with his fingers, Italian style—"wow!"

Blessed Sloth

"I lead a very disciplined life. I'm up at six-thirty. I exercise, shave, shower, eat, and I'm off to my office, the same time every weekday, and my work is routine. I come home at the same time and my evening routine is disciplined too," Greg tells me. "With that kind of day-to-day life, my greatest pleasure is slothfulness."

I smile, not quite understanding him. At fifty-two, gray-haired and elegantly dressed, Greg looks the stereotype of the successful businessman—which he is.

"How do you mean, slothfulness?" I ask.

"I take a month's vacation each year. The last two weeks are for Eloise. We try to fly to Paris, or tour through Europe, but the first two weeks are mine."

"What do you do?"

"We have a cabin in Maine. It used to be great when the kids were young and we couldn't afford to travel, but now I only use it for those two weeks each year. I go up there, usually alone because Eloise can't face it, and I slip into slothfulness."

"How?"

"Well, to begin with, I don't shave. I wear old, comfortable clothes. I do exactly what I want to do. If you want to use the new psychological jargon, I spend an unconstructed two weeks. I sleep as late as I wish. In the beginning that's hard. I find I'm automatically waking up at six-thirty, but then I can go back to sleep and doze until I'm hungry. After a few days my body clock unwinds and I find that I can sleep till ten and even eleven.

"I get up when I feel like it, and often as not I read in bed in the morning."

"That's a new one on me."

"Isn't it? I often read myself to sleep, but never quite as late as I'd like to at home. Up in the cabin—well, I'll read till two or three in the morning if I feel like it, and if I'm too lazy to get out of bed when I wake up, I just reach out for my book and glasses and start reading again.

"And there's another thing. I'm slothful in my reading up there. I stay away from 'good' books or educational books and I just take along entertainment, stuff I read for fun.

"When I do get up I eat exactly what I want to, and when I want to. Forget about three meals a day. If I want six, I eat six—how much weight can you put on in two weeks?

"And anyway, it all balances out. There are some days when I just don't feel like eating at all, so I don't. Occasionally I'll take a steak out of the freezer and have that—just that and no more, no potatoes, no salad, no vegetables—no goddamned balanced meals!"

He laughs. "I'm sorry. I forget myself, but you see that's the real pleasure. I don't worry about scurvy or rickets, I eat what I like when I like to. Some evenings I build a fire and stretch out in the easy chair with a book and a bottle of Irish whiskey and sip or drink."

"Do you ever get out of the cabin?"

"Oh, sure. I hike in the woods, or if the mood takes me I drive into town in the evening and see a movie, or drop into a bar and listen to the locals. It's fun listening as long as I remember not to open my mouth.

"The point is, I spend two undisciplined weeks doing what I want to do, not what my family and the world expect me to do.

"You know, that cabin has a sun deck and a little lawn usually overgrown with weeds. Last summer, in the middle of my days of sloth, I wandered out on the sun deck and thought, Hey—why not take a sunbath without clothes? There was no one within sight. So I did and I loved it—and then I began to think, That lawn needs mowing. So I got out the mower and, still in the raw, I mowed it.

"While I was doing it I got a glimpse of myself in the glass window of the cabin and I couldn't stop laughing. It looked so incongruous, but what the hell—I wanted to do it so I did it!

"Those two weeks are a combination of sloth and impulse. I want to do something? As long as it doesn't hurt anyone else I do it. I want to take a nap at noon? Swell, I take it. I want to go without showering or shaving? That's okay too. On the other hand, anytime I want I can run myself a nice hot bath and soak in it as long as I want.

"The joy comes from the absolute lack of rules, and along with that goes a lack of anxiety, a lack of tension and drive. No matter how erratically I eat during that time, my stomach behaves perfectly. No antacids or aspirins up in my cabin.

"You know, I have a theory that our gut is the key to inner peace—forget about psychoanalysis and meditation. When we're at peace our gut goes through its paces perfectly. When we're disturbed, it's disturbed. The fact that mine doesn't ever give me a hint of trouble during those two weeks convinces me that if I eat a meal of ice cream and beer, or a salami sandwich, it won't affect my digestion. I can function beautifully.

"What does affect me, no matter how I eat, is the discipline of ordinary, everyday life. That's why I get so much pleasure when I discard it and sink into blessed sloth!"

All Things Wild and Wonderful

The Qantas Airlines commercial comes on the television screen and Barbara, a grown woman, cries out like a child at the sight of the koala bear.

"Have you ever seen a live one?" I ask her.

"Oh, yes, when I was in Australia. I was a teen-ager, but I've never forgotten it. My children tease me about the fun I get out of watching them. They even bought me a stuffed koala, and it's funny—I get a kick out of that too."

"As much as the real thing?"

"Of course not." She pushes her hair back, smiling. "I don't know why I get so much pleasure out of watching animals, but there's just something about them that turns me on."

"What is it?"

"Their grace?" she says hesitantly. "When we're out driving around dusk I keep looking for deer. The other evening we passed a spot in the new state park, a deserted meadow, and we saw a herd of ten deer. I felt such a thrill I just got gooseflesh all over. They're so beautiful, so graceful . . . so right!"

"Right?"

"Yes, they give me a feeling that they just *belong*. They have that incredible stillness before they move, as if they're somehow frozen in time. Their innocence makes you aware that this is the way all animals should be—maybe the way men should be too. I don't know if I'm making myself clear, but there's so much beauty in a wild animal."

"Do you find the same beauty in animals in zoos?"

"Oh, I hate zoos. Although in some—well, I must admit I enjoyed watching Patty Cake, the baby gorilla in the New York Central Park Zoo. They had her in a cage with a chimp, and she was so slow, so gentle compared to the chimp. I just wanted to pick her up and cuddle her. Some animals arouse a maternal pleasure in me—the koalas and pandas, for example. I dragged my husband out to the London zoo six years ago to see the panda, and all it did was sleep in the grass.

"I was disappointed, but then last year we went to Washington to see the two new young pandas. They were so lively, so full of mischief and tricks—but you get an entirely different pleasure out of watching animals in captivity. It's not like seeing them in the wild."

"Are there that many wild animals left to see?"

"Are you joking? Of course there are. We spent a week at a hotel in the mountains and each night we'd feed leftover food to a family of raccoons that lived under the porch. They were wild, but they'd eat out of our hands.

"I loved it every time one snatched a piece of food out of my hand and nibbled at it. That same summer we used to drive to the garbage dumps to see the bears rummage through the debris. They had their own grace, a clumsy kind, but the grace of the wild. That was the summer we saw a fox run across the road, a real wild fox with its bushy tail lifted and its pointy snout. And then there are all the critters . . ."

"Critters? What are they?"

"Well, you see them nibbling grass at the side of the road when you drive along. We call them critters, maybe they're beavers or woodchucks or badgers—I don't know. They're small and brown and adorable. And the national parks! In Yellowstone we watched a moose just a few feet away in the shallows of a stream.

"Some wild animals, like the raccoon, are born clowns—begging food, turning over garbage cans. Some, like the skunks, are so arrogant they'll walk right under a car on the road. And possums—they really do play dead. Then in another park out West we stopped near a herd of wild burros, and while I was feeding one, another started nudging me.

"It's funny, but a lot of our family trips have been involved with animals. What I would really like to see, though, is wild wolves. I think I'd be terribly scared, but it would be worth it. I've read about them and I know they're not the monsters books make them out to be. Do you know they mate for life?"

"Would you want a wild-animal pet, a tame wolf or deer?"

"Oh, no. How terrible. Don't you see, the real pleasure of animals is in seeing them where they belong, in their own habitats. That's when they're complete and beautiful. Maybe I'm basically a voyeur—an animal voyeur—but watching them where they belong is my greatest pleasure."

The Best of the Grape

"My first experience with wine," Jack tells me, "came when I was just a child. My father took a heavy, sweet wine made out of Málaga grapes, added some soda and ice, and I had a grape soda. I grew up thinking, 'That was wine? Who needs it?'"

"When did you discover real wine?"

"I didn't really think about wine until I was in my thirties. Oh, I drank it, but till then I never considered drinking it a pleasant experience. It was just another food, hardly strong enough to get you drunk. I started with cold white wines. They were easy to take, and after a while I grew to appreciate them.

"But it wasn't until I began drinking red wines that weren't chilled that I realized how much pleasure was involved."

"Why red wines?"

"They have more taste. They should be served at room temperature. A chilled wine sort of anesthetizes the taste buds. At room temperature, a wine enhances the flavor of everything you eat. Then, too, it creates a certain atmosphere at a meal. There's an esthetic pleasure to its color.

"You know, I'm no tremendous wine authority. I just like wines. They give me pleasure, but once you've tasted the good red wines, you search for even more expensive ones. Then you hit that moment when you drink a really great wine, a Lafite or a Latour from a grand year, and you understand what it's all about. Coming upon that tremendous flavor is a pure sensual treat."

"Is that the greatest pleasure, the flavor?"

"Not entirely. There should be a perfect balance of aroma —that's very important—and taste, and there should be no aftertaste. Then you know you've hit a fine wine!

"An authority can tell the difference between châteaux. I can't, but I can tell the difference between a good wine and a great one. It's tremendous. Sure, a good wine gives you pleasure. It tastes good and helps the meal, but a great wine! That's a rarity. If you drank a bottle of such a wine every night it would pall on you. That's why its scarcity contributes to the pleasure. So does recognition."

"Recognition?"

"Sure. When I find a great wine for the second time, it's like meeting an old friend. There's that delight of recognition when I drink it." He shrugs. "I think there's more pleasure in recognizing it than in drinking it, if you're a real wine lover.

"Once you get into wine drinking," he goes on, "you become intrigued with this recognition aspect. It can easily become a habit. You begin to understand your own ability to recognize and identify wines. The next step is drinking wine without a meal, drinking as you'd drink a cocktail. You very quickly lose your taste for mixed drinks.

"And after that"—he shakes his head—"you're lost. You tailor your meal to suit your wine instead of selecting the wine to match the meal."

"How do you mean?"

"Well, my wife and I have had bread and cheese alone when we had a particularly good wine, and it was a fine meal. With a great wine you find that you want to eat very plain food so you don't spoil the taste of the wine."

"What about the California wines? Do they give you the same pleasure?"

He hesitates. "I know there's a lot of snobbishness about wines, but to tell you the truth, I've never had a California wine to compare with even a medium French one. And the best French wine—well, it's just so far ahead of California's.

"Now New York State makes a good champagne, close to a French champagne, but then champagne is a blend of wines. A château wine is a blend of grapes. There are so many facets to winemaking, so many influences—the soil, the sun, the fertilizer, and, of course, the winemaker.

"I've had good Italian wines and some good Spanish ones, but none of them are as complex as the French. For real pleasure, give me a French wine anytime."

"How much of the pleasure in drinking wine is the alcoholic content?"

"I'm not sure. I might enjoy it without the alcohol, but would it taste the same? I don't drink wine to get drunk, but part of the total complex of wine drinking, part of the pleasure you get is that soft alcoholic glow.

"You know, there's a danger in this pleasure that I should warn you about."

"What's that?"

"Well, I drink wine with every meal, and each year I want a better wine. It can become an expensive taste. There's always the danger that the desire to acquire a better wine can become the major part of the pleasure. Then the wine drinking is controlling you. You're not controlling it."

He shakes his head. "The best bottle of wine I ever had was a 1953 Château Lafite. It takes twenty years for true maturity, and that wine was mature! I tell you, the moment I tasted it and realized that it was better than any wine I ever had before—that was such utter pleasure that I still remember it.

"Now, what I really hope to find is a '45 Lafite, a great rarity, but if I find it I think I'll buy it, no matter what the price—and don't think there isn't pleasure in just anticipating that bottle!"

Mind-tripping

The other day I picked up a medical journal with an article devoted to the problem-solving benefits of daydreaming. A study of three hundred college students showed that those who tended to daydream were quicker at solving problems and better able to handle crises than their sober classmates. Daydreaming, the article concluded, was a form of internal rehearsal. Dreaming up a problem and solving it mentally was a step toward someday solving it for real.

I put down the journal with mixed feelings. As a confirmed daydreamer I was glad to know I was doing something valuable. At the same time, I felt the article had overlooked something important: the pleasure of daydreaming. What about the sheer fun you can get by creating other worlds and stepping into them?

I remember my most satisfying daydream. I was ten or eleven, and I had just had the most miserable day of my life, what with a failing report card from school, a fight with my brothers, and the loss of my after-school job.

It was a rainy autumn day and I took a long walk in the park. The rain stopped and the mist drifted across the path in gray tattered shreds; there was no hint of sun. Suddenly the empty park reminded me of a desolate landscape described in one of the Oz books I had read. How great it would be if I were transported to Oz! Although I was too old to put any hope in that, it was easy for me to people the park with characters from the Oz stories. I daydreamed as I walked, creating my own happy fantasy; the images were easily evoked by the rain-swept solitude and mist around me.

In minutes I was outside of home, school, job, and well into pleasant fantasy. My daydream got me through that day, turning disaster into pleasure. Perhaps it didn't help solve my overall problems, but it did give me a breathing space—and a pleasant one.

Even then, I was an old hand at using fantasy to get pleasure. Children use their imagination naturally. I've seen my kids sit for hours playing "little people," a microcosm game in which an entire village can be compacted into one square foot with stones for houses and twigs for people. Sometimes a city, or even a world, can fit into a back yard. The rules are elastic—whatever you wish to happen happens. You have control, complete and absolute.

Control is one of the most pleasant elements of fantasy. When we fantasize we make things happen exactly as we wish them to be. We remold reality "nearer to the heart's desire." We win all our battles, achieve all our goals, find fame and fortune, bypass all the suffering and strain. What does it matter if the achievements are all gone in an hour or so? In our daydreams we have happiness, and we can return to it at any time.

I have a friend whose whole family is caught up in daydreams. They buy sweepstakes tickets and spend hours discussing what they'll spend their winnings on—the things they'll buy, the places they'll visit.

"But you all know how slim your chances of winning are," I protested after an evening at my friend's house. "How can you waste all that time making such elaborate plans?"

"It's no waste." He shook his head. "We enjoy the planning, the spending, and the dreams. We all know we won't win—but what fun it is to daydream about winning!"

When I told the story to another friend, she nodded. "I understand just how they feel. I'm an armchair traveler. I've made itineraries for a hundred trips to every part of the world. I send for travel folders and brochures. Sure, I know the odds against my going anywhere are tremendous. I just don't have that kind of money, but I get so much pleasure out of planning the trip that I really don't mind not going."

Another friend who confided that he's a frequent daydreamer told me, "It's better than reading."

"How so?"

"With books I'm restricted to the author's imagination and I know that's all it is—imagination. In a daydream I can do things my way. There are no restrictions, no rules or regulations. Anything can happen—anything wonderful and exciting. I work out literally hundreds of stories in my own mind."

"You sound as if you'd be a good novelist."

"Maybe, but I'd hate it. For my own stories, told to and for myself, I have one devoted fan—me. I don't have to please anyone else. I don't have to worry about reviews or sales. I'm my own audience. I can be as nice or as nasty as I want. No, I wouldn't give up my daydreams for anything!" He patted his ample stomach. "Look, in my dreams I can be as slim as I like—without dieting —and I can always get the girl!"

Impressed by his intensity, I've revived some daydreaming techniques from my childhood. To start, you must relax, if not physically, at least mentally. A bus or a train is a perfect place to daydream, but almost any place will do. You can even daydream while walking. Think of a favorite situation from a book or movie and put in all the variations that please you. Then put yourself in the scene. Carry it along in whatever direction you wish, to whatever end you want. I often find it difficult to dream during the day, but at night, in the moments before sleep comes, I daydream extravagantly. I started it one night when I was plagued by insomnia. My fantasies didn't put me to sleep—I was up half the night—but it was a pleasant time. I simply relaxed and let the daydream take over, leading me wherever it went. When at last I fell asleep, I felt no anxiety about having lost sleep. I had enjoyed every minute of my daydream.

Turn, Turn, Turn

"The thing I can't stand about Southern California," Vera said violently, "is that there isn't a single deciduous tree around!"

We had been talking about the difficulty of adjusting to Hollywood, and Vera's vehemence took me by surprise. "What's that got to do with it?"

"It's just that around this time of year, near the middle of October, I get a yen to see autumn. To walk though the woods and see the autumn coloring—oh, I miss it so!"

I thought of Vera last autumn as I drove through Vermont, and I realized how much pleasure I took in the changing of the seasons. The incredible reds and oranges of the maples, the vivid yellow of the poplars, the copper and bronze of the oaks and nut trees, were unforgettable against the intense blue autumn sky.

With autumn, too, I always think of the smell of burning leaves and long walks through the changing woods, rides into the country to see the change, to check this year's color against last's—to me, autumn is all color and odor.

My friend Alex agrees with me. "But I really dig winter," he tells me. "I take my vacation in January and I drive up to the mountains. Not for the skiing but for the winter countryside. Have you ever walked through the woods after a snowfall? Everything is white and clean, and there are patterns to everything."

"Patterns?"

"Sure. The tree trunks against the snow. The snow on the branches. The frozen brooks and streams—I once spent half an hour sitting by a stream in the dead of winter watching the way the water ran under the ice, and the patterns the ice made. And did you ever realize that winter is the only time of year that you can really see the shape of a tree's branches? The upsweep of an elm, the symmetry of a maple—they're hidden by leaves in the other seasons.

"I also love the cleanness and sharpness of winter. Every sound is clearer, more perfect, as if the cold sharpens tone and pitch. And even in the city, for a little while after a snowfall, everything is clean and neat and beautiful. I've seen piles of garbage softened and dignified by snow."

Mike, who's been listening to us, says, "Let me put in my vote for summer. No matter how beautiful the woods are in autumn and winter, they're in their real glory during the summer. Have you ever noticed how many shades of green there are? I can look at any patch of forest and see literally dozens of different tones of that one color, and even the same green is different at different times of day.

"In summer I think of the woods as cathedrals, green roofs of leaves and Gothic arches of tree trunks, and the blue sky like stained glass. And then in the middle of all that are splashes of color, the blues and yellows and violets of the wildflowers."

"They are different from the autumn colors," I agree.

"The colors of summer are alive," Mike goes on. "They're bright and translucent and subtle. Autumn is a riot of undisciplined color."

Joanna reminds us of the beauty of spring. "I love to see

everything just waking up, when the leaves are unfolding and the snow melting. It's a time of rebirth, rediscovery—it makes me feel extra alive."

I realize that we've all been talking about change, the pleasure of change. There's a Gilbert and Sullivan lyric that goes, "Summer if eternal makes the roses fade." Well, what would summer be if it weren't for the contrast of winter? How boring the day would be without the night, how dull the ocean without the changing tides—and without rain, snow, or sleet, the sunshine would be unbearable.

Reflections from an Inner Tube

"Here's another cut." Gravely, Jules inspects his hands. "I tore my nail here, and my wedding ring was shoved into my finger—that's just oozing, not really bleeding."

"There's a black and blue mark on your leg and another out there," I tell him. "I think you'll feel that when the chill of the water wears off. Was it really worth it?"

Jules has just traveled two miles of the Esopus creek in an inner tube, his bottom seated in the middle, his legs and arms hanging over the sides. "Worth it? Why, sure. I had a marvelous time. We shot five sets of white-water rapids, and that's really great."

"But dangerous?"

"Well, yes. You know, there's always a moment when you suddenly realize that you have no control over the tube. It's going along with you inside it, and no matter how you splash or paddle, it keeps going. That's a frightening moment, but it's an exciting one."

"Is it really so pleasant?"

"Oh, yes! To me, pleasure is always much more intense when it's side by side with danger or excitement. You get into a stretch of white water, bobbing along like a cork with no real protection, and you feel a breathless moment of panic that's the very essence of pleasure.

"And, of course, it isn't all white water. You'll come out of a stretch of rapids and the creek will broaden out and become like a small lake, flowing very gently, the banks thick with willow and wild mint and piles of red and green shale pebbles. Then I lean back in the tube and let it spin slowly, look up at the sky and the mountains and the trees and watch the dragonflies zip across the water. Sometimes I'll look down and if it's clear enough I'll see a trout hovering along the bottom, its nose upstream. Today, only a few feet away from me, I saw a red-winged blackbird swinging on a branch.

"There's an exquisite sense of calm. Everything is slow and gentle and you get a different perspective of things. You see the land from the water—not the usual view of the water from the land. The reflections ripple and shine. They're so fascinating because you're in them!

"Then, just as you're getting your breath and beginning to relax, you swing around and find yourself up against another set of rapids. Each one is different, and each one seems to have a distinct personality. I went over one so shallow that I was barely able to float, and there was the constant danger of slamming my butt against a rock or bruising my arms and legs. You have to arch your back, but that throws your balance off and you're much more vulnerable to upset.

"Then there was another stretch of white water much deeper. I cleared the rocks easily but the water raced along and I really had to fight to stay right side up. I knew if I could stay that way I was okay, but I was balancing every inch of the way. What a triumph when I made it safely!

"Sometimes there's no problem at all. The water rushes along, but all you have to do is paddle occasionally to keep on course. Then you have the sense of surface motion, of rushing along with the river. There's a tremendous pleasure in that.

"I don't know which part of the whole trip was the most fun,"

Jules says thoughtfully as he patches the cuts and scratches on his body with Band-Aids, "the visual excitement of the land and water, the trees and mountains and sky—the beauty of it all—or the excitement of being flung down the rapids, the sense of motion, racing along or the lack of control, the realization that the river is bigger, tougher, and stronger than you are.

"That's another thing. Just an hour or so on a trip like that gives you a different perspective of nature. You're suddenly brought face to face with her strength."

"And that's pleasant?"

"Yes, because with it comes belonging. To make the trip down the creek, you have to put yourself in the hands of nature. You get through and you feel, Well, I've done it. I'm a part of that creek. Nature's allowed me to make the trip."

I shake my head. "But what if you don't make it?"

"Oh, the odds are so good that I don't even consider that. Sure it's dangerous, but there's danger everywhere. It simply makes the pleasure keener—like salt with meat." He winces suddenly. "Oh-oh. I can't see back there. Is it a bruise or a cut?"

The Evocative Pleasure

"About two years ago I heard of a store out in the suburbs that made its own ice cream. I drove twelve miles, got lost three times, and wound up with a traffic ticket for going through a red light. But I found my store, a seedy little candy shop that hadn't been redecorated since nineteen-oh-something. It still had its original marble soda bar—and the ice cream!" Max, a thin, ascetic-looking man in his early thirties, casts his eyes heavenward. "It was superb. It had a combination of creaminess and richness and smoothness that screamed 'homemade!' There were only three flavors, vanilla, strawberry, and chocolate—but what a vanilla! Oh, my, that's a pleasure I still taste."

Max is an ice-cream freak. As we sit talking in the park on a hot summer day, a man comes by pushing an ice-cream cart. I look at it wistfully, but Max shakes his head.

"In the first place," he says, "those pops they sell are only good for two bites. In the second place, they're not really ice cream. They're some plastic goo whipped and frozen and covered with God-awful toppings of crushed this-and-that.

"Ice cream should be plain, without whipped cream, nuts, sauce or marshmallow. How can you taste the flavor with all that stuff on it?"

"Speaking of flavor," I say, "a friend of mine who is a big wine buff claims that cold anesthetizes the taste buds. If that's true, how can ice cream have any flavor?"

"There's a simple answer."

"Yes?"

"It's not true. Look, no matter what your experts tell you, the truth is that cold—I don't mean intense cold, but the cold you feel in a spoonful of ice cream—actually stimulates the taste buds. It's a scientific fact that it cools off certain highly irritable elements in the tasting apparatus and allows the part of the tongue responsible for analyzing taste to operate more effectively."

"You're saying the sense of taste improves with cold?"

"Right on. More discriminating is the way I'd describe it. That's why I love ice cream so. Not only does the cold affect the taste buds, but it affects the ingredients in the ice cream as well. The cold makes the flavorings more subtle. Chewing a vanilla bean isn't all that pleasant, but flecks of real vanilla bean in ice cream are exquisite."

"You're a real ice-cream maven."

"No. That implies an authority—the judgmental approach of saying this brand is better than that. I'm a lover of all ice cream. I can't think of any pleasure greater than a bowl of good ice cream in the right surroundings."

"Are surroundings that important?"

"You'd better believe it. Someone opened a store downtown called the Ice Cream Parlor, and decorated it like an old-fashioned soda fountain with Tiffany lights, a marble counter, and wrought-iron chairs. No wonder it's mobbed. The surroundings add that psychological touch that enhances the gustatory delight of eating."

"That sounds complicated."

"Not at all. You have to understand that ice cream is an evocative food. I take a spoonful of rich vanilla and close my eyes and I taste straw boaters and twilight in a small town, broad green lawns and porches with lanterns and laughter drifting out to the street, girls in floor-length skirts and white blouses with their hair tied back in broad ribbons and men in striped blazers—I taste Main Street and soda fountains with the scent of sarsaparilla and root beer . . ."

"All that in a spoonful of ice cream?"

"Of course, and the better the ice cream, the clearer the vision. I'm not so much concerned with the purity of the product as with the taste—cold, creamy, rich, with no hint of ice. That's one easy way to tell a good from a bad ice cream. If you taste the ice crystals, forget it.

"I suppose it's a matter of technique more than ingredients, but if the result is right, I can close my eyes and see an old-fashioned wooden ice-cream freezer being turned in the shade of a back-yard maple tree with a couple of small kids salivating expectantly."

"What about sherbet?"

"Oh, I like sherbet, but it's a different thing. Ices too, and ice milk—each has its place, but none is ice cream. I separate true ice cream from all the weight-watching products and frozen yoghurt—which, incidentally, is all filler. I don't mind the fillers, but in truth, you can usually taste the difference. Once you taste a pure, homemade ice cream, nothing else tastes quite as wonderful."

"But you don't like sundaes?"

"When I was a kid I used to go the fudge-nut-marshmallow route, but as I grew older and developed a palate I began to zero in on the plainer, more exacting freezes. I like Baskin-Robbins and Howard Johnson too, but who needs all those flavors? I could be happy with only vanilla. If I needed another flavor, there are other basics, chocolate and strawberry—beyond that I can get all the variety I need from the nuts, butter pecan, pistachio, maple walnut."

"What about coffee? That's my favorite."

"Oh, yes. Oddly enough, coffee can take a bit of enhancement. Try it with a dollop of Tía María."

"Is ice cream as American as apple pie?"

"No, it's international. But, you know, I've traveled all through Europe and even those countries known for ice cream can't match the stuff that's made here in the States. Russia has good ice cream, and Italy isn't bad, but I was disappointed in France and England and even in the Scandinavian countries.

"One of the big troubles with the ice-cream field is that the knack of packing ice cream has been forgotten. The quick-serve chains weigh it, and it's packed so loosely you always feel cheated. In the old days they used to put the container in a metal mold, and then pack it in till the metal couldn't hold any more. I was always amazed at how much they kept packing in. Those were the days when ice-cream clerks had muscles in their forearms. They needed them in order to pack properly.

"Now they hire school kids who weigh it." He shakes his head sadly. "That's why ambience is so important. When I find an old-fashioned-looking ice-cream parlor and a clerk with muscular forearms, I know I'm in for a treat."

The Music
of the Spheres

"There's a fantastic pleasure in being literally wrapped in sound, in having it go through your flesh and bones until your entire body is reverberating. You close your eyes and all your other senses are blacked out. There's only the perception of sound, but on a level above hearing. It's in your very being, but it has to be experienced to be understood."

Dick looks at me with excitement in his eyes, but I am bewildered. "Where can you experience that?" I ask.

"Where else but in a bell tower when a carillon is being rung?"

"You have to explain that."

"Well, let's see—a few years ago someone came up with the bright idea of ringing church bells all over the country at a r.m. on the Fourth of July. Now Riverside Church in New York City has a carillon of five bells. All of them are arranged so that they can be played from a keyboard—they're moved by a hydraulic motor. They sound the hour and the quarter hour with the theme from *Parsifal*.

"The biggest bell in the Riverside carillon, the boudin, rings C below middle C, and at its mouth it's twelve feet across. The clapper alone weighs over a ton! The bells are up in the steeple, twenty stories above the ground. You take an elevator up and then you have to climb the last five flights in the bell tower. Then you go out on a catwalk and right in front of you is the boudin bell.

"Well, I went up there on the Fourth and stood on the catwalk. I felt a shiver go through me as the bells began to swing back and forth, and then the clapper came up and struck the side. The smaller bells were hit first and their higher notes started the song. Then that giant clapper swung up, the mouth of the bell turned toward me, so huge! And it hit."

"What was it like?"

"It was the most wonderful sound I've ever heard. Not only the basic note, but the octave and the fifth, the third and the fourth —you know, each bell is tuned to strike a particular note, but there are overtones, and they come almost at random."

"Isn't it cacophonous?"

"No. It's melodic and pleasant," Dick assures me. "When that bell sounds you can shout as loud as you want and the person next to you can't hear you. You stay there for five minutes and it becomes a fantastic, crazy experience . . . just wild!"

He laughs. "You actually seem to vibrate with the sound, inside and outside. It's all around you. You can't help yourself, you just shout out with laughter. It's all so pleasant and such abandon—and all-absorbing too. You're isolated from the world by noise that seems almost solid."

"Have you gone up there often?"

"Every year since then. It's a pleasure I look forward to all year."

"But isn't sound like that dangerous? Wasn't there a Dorothy Sayers mystery where a man was killed by the vibrations of a bell?"

"Yes, *The Nine Tailors*, and she's probably right. It might kill you if it were carried on for a long time in a closed-in space. But remember, up there you're in an open bell tower, not cooped up, and you're only there for five minutes. There's no feeling of fear when you experience it." He shakes his head. "The only thing I was afraid of was that that crazy clapper would come off. Imagine a ton of metal crashing through that tower!

"You know, you mentioned the Dorothy Sayers book. That's what really made me so aware of the bells. I read the book when I was in college. Our chapel had a peal of bells with fourteen notes. For two years I had the job of playing it every morning before chapel as well as afternoons and Sundays. I loved it.

"Then I read the Sayers book, and I became fascinated with change ringing—you know, the ringing of tuned bells in a continually changing order. I read up on the subject and worked out a set of changes to play on the college peal. I played them one afternoon."

"What sort of reaction did you get?"

"Everyone thought I was crazy. A change sounds like noise, not music. You have to be educated to appreciate it. But I enjoyed it. But being under and close to the bells is a different sort of pleasure. You aren't really aware of music or notes, only of that incredible reverberation. You close your eyes and it's heavenly. That's when you truly feel the music of the spheres!"

To Shop, Perchance to Dream

"What I really love," Gwen tells me one day when a group of us are rapping about pleasure, "is to go downtown and window-shop. I get a tremendous amount of pleasure out of just looking in the different store windows, at the jewelry, clothing, and appliances."

"Don't you want to buy them?"

"No—not really. I get my jollies out of looking. Buying?" Gwen shrugs. "I'm always anxious when I have to shop. I think maybe I'm spending too much money, or what I buy isn't worth what I pay—but window-shopping's different. In a way it's like visiting a museum. You don't have to own the exhibits to enjoy them. Just looking at them is pleasure in itself, and it's the same with store windows.

"You know, I even enjoy looking in the windows of liquor

shops. I'm no lush, but I get a real fantasy trip out of reading the labels on the wine bottles—don't laugh, they have a lot of romance there. All those foreign names and places—French, Italian, Spanish, Israeli, Chilean—it's the same pleasure I get out of reading a travel supplement.

"Candy shops too." Gwen pats her ample hips. "Not that I'd ever dream of going in and buying candy, but I get a vicarious thrill out of looking."

Helen nods. "I can understand that. I get my kicks out of going into stores and pricing things—especially clothing stores. Of course, it's a little more than window-shopping. There's always the possibility that I might find something I really want or an irresistible bargain. I love browsing through racks of marked-down clothes, and my antennae perk up when I see 'Final Clearance.' It's like searching for the impossible dream. I always expect to find that one great buy, that fabulous dress in just my size and the style I love marked down to practically nothing.

"Then, too, it's a way of being with a lot of people without having to relate to any of them."

Surprised, I ask, "Do you get pleasure out of that?"

Helen shrugs. "I suppose it's unusual but it makes me feel sort of—safe. When I'm shopping I'm surrounded by people. I'm not alone, and yet I don't have to make the effort to talk to any of them."

We're silent for a moment, and then Gwen says, "Another thing I enjoy is going through the furniture departments of the really fancy department stores. Many of them have sample rooms set up. Their decorators are usually very good and I get all sorts of ideas—even if I don't get to use any."

Helen nods. "I do the same with clothes. I like to put on my best outfit and visit one of the most expensive boutiques in town and try on all the lovely Pucci's and Dior's. I'll usually pick tiny faults with each to justify my not buying it."

Jane and her husband have been listening quietly, and now Jane laughs. "You have to be careful when you play that game. Do it too often in the same store and they'll freeze you out."

Helen agrees. "And there's another danger. Sometimes you try on the absolutely perfect dress and wow—that's it. The temptation is more than you can stand, and you figure, What if I really splurged, just once?"

Elmer, Jane's husband, says, "You know, this game isn't limited to women alone. I don't go for trying on clothes, but my son and I love to stop at automobile lots when we have absolutely no intention of buying. We'll see what we can get on a trade-in for our old heap against the best model in the house. We bargain like crazy and, you know, when you have no intention of buying you can do a fantastic bargaining number. It's great to get down to a rock-bottom price, then turn it down."

Gwen says, "My husband does that with boats. He's always wanted one but we could never afford it. He has fun pricing them and talking over the different features with the salesmen."

"Now that I think of it," Helen puts in, "my husband and I have been doing a variation of that for years. We've been shopping for a summer house since the kids were born, but to tell the truth, it's all window-shopping. Each Sunday we drive out to a new area and let the real-estate people take us around from house to house. It's such fun to imagine what our lives would be like if we had the place—I'd almost hate to end it all by actually buying."

"Elmer and I spent last month shopping for swimming pools," Jane admits. "The in-ground pools are terribly expensive, but we've found some very reasonable aboveground models."

"But you live in an apartment," Helen protests.

Jane shrugs. "What's the difference when you're window-shopping?"

Wonderful Weeds

"A weed is simply a wildflower growing in the wrong place," Alan tells me. "Plant it where you want it, nurture it, and it rewards you with the beauty of a flower. It may be small and delicate or big and ornate, but it's always pretty.

"I enjoy wildflowers. I get a tremendous amount of pleasure out of finding them and identifying them, but most of my pleasure comes from just seeing them. I enjoy their beauty, color, shape, and delicacy. That's why I feel so strongly about weeds. They bring a touch of pleasure to the most unlikely places because they'll grow where nothing else will—in empty lots in the city, through cracks in the pavement, and anywhere that there's a patch of dirt.

"You know, I've found all sorts of wildflowers right in the heart of the city. Knotweed for one, with its knots of pink and purple little blossoms. It gets a foothold where nothing else will bother to grow. Then there's mullein. It has tall spikes with yellow flowers and great big hairy leaves. The kids call them elephant ears. One of my favorites is bladder campion, with its little white flowers. Sure, they're all weeds, but I love seeing them."

"Do you enjoy them just because they don't seem to belong in the city?"

Alan nods. "That's a big part of it, but I also feel they're old friends. I know wildflowers very well because I've always enjoyed them and I deliberately set out to learn their names. That changed everything for me."

"In what way?"

He spreads his hands. "Well, it gave me a greater appreciation of the beauty of green things. Maybe it's because I'm a city boy that greenery is so precious to me. But when I find a little patch of ground all covered with weeds, I bend down and separate the weeds into individuals. Sometimes I find sorrel with its little rusty flowers and its sour-tasting leaves. Or plaintain—you have to look sharp to notice that its flowers aren't just stems but tiny delicate blooms on green spikes.

"And then I get a great deal of pleasure out of identifying different plants for my friends. Maybe it's an ego trip, but I enjoy it."

"Are you only interested in city flowers?"

"Oh, no," Alan protests. "It's lots of fun recognizing wild-flowers in the heart of the city, but it can't compare to the pleasure of seeing wildflowers out in the country, where they grow in such profusion. Sometimes I'll be driving along a country road and I'll see banks and banks of blue chicory, or a field of milkweed with its dusty rose-colored blossom—incidentally, much sweeter and more cloying than roses. Milkweed must have the strongest wildflower scent there is.

"Or I'll come on a meadow full of daisies, or a hill covered with goldenrod, such splashes of color against the green! Or wild mint, bergamot—you'll see a whole field of it, violet and pink—but you'll smell it first.

"And of course the same flowers that are such hesitant ghosts in the city are in their glory in the country. They have room to grow without fighting tar and concrete, so their blossoms are bigger and more colorful." He hesitates. "And there's the matter of light."

"Light?"

"Well, let me try to explain. In the city, what with the smog and the dirt, you never get the clear sweet air you can find in the country. I mean, sometimes you'll come on a patch of flowers growing in the woods, where the light is turned to green by the leaves of the trees, and everything is silent—seeing wildflowers like that is almost a religious experience.

"Or seeing them on a hillside where the sun drenches them with brilliance, or in a little cleft in the hills where the light is bright but diffused—there are so many different kinds of light in nature. From moment to moment a flower changes as the light changes.

"And that too is part of the pleasure of wildflowers. You see a group of familiar flowers, but you realize that somehow they're different, and then you realize it's the day and the clouds and the light.

"I also get such pleasure out of the difference in wildflowers. You know, there are so many kinds I don't think I could ever learn all of them. In North America alone there are almost eight thousand different species—and each has its season. You see most of them in the spring, but there's never a part of summer without flowers. And even when the flowers are gone, there are often brilliant berries or fascinating seed pods that last through the winter. If you take a walk in November or December you'll see the delicate stalks and outlines of flowers you probably didn't even notice during the summer. In fact, some of my favorite wildflower bouquets were made up of the dry winter plants. In their own way they're as lovely as bunches of wildflowers in their prime."

"I remember the fun of picking flowers when I was a kid, but they never seemed to last."

"If you pick them at the right time of day and get them quickly into water they'll last," he tells me. "But they never seem right in a house. They're at their best in the woods or in open meadows or alongside a road where everyone can enjoy them. A few weeks ago, driving in the country, we took a road whose banks were carpeted with Queen Anne's lace. It was like driving through a cloud. I finally had to stop just to stare at them, the pleasure of seeing them was that intense."

Mantra Magic

Alex meditates in the morning, at night, and when he can spare a moment or two during the day. I meet him at the gym for a grueling workout, followed by a visit to the sauna. There Alex goes into the lotus position and with an apologetic smile drifts off.

When he comes out of it, I ask him, "Do you get much pleasure out of meditation?"

"I do. I find it very relaxing, physically relaxing, and that's pleasant."

"What exactly is transcendental meditation?"

"What it says," Alex replies. "Meditation that tries to transcend our earthly bonds. You know, in deep meditation, you get a feeling of suspended animation—how can I put it? As if you were inside a bell jar. Everything around you is muted by that jar."

"Do you need the right surroundings to meditate?"

He shakes his head. "You saw me meditate here in the sauna. I can meditate on a train with all the racket going on, or just as easily when it's completely quiet. I simply cover myself with that bell jar, no matter where I am."

"I've tried," I confess, "and my thoughts get in the way."

He shrugs. "I literally see my thoughts floating through my head. You see, the method is based on a mantra, a mystical formula in Sanskrit. I keep repeating it, and it keeps interacting with my thoughts. The thoughts recede and then come forward."

"I find it very hard not thinking," I say.

"But in a sense I still think while I meditate. I reach a certain level, depending on my powers of concentration, and then a pleasant feeling, a relaxed feeling, goes all through me.

"My whole body is at such a low level of metabolism, if I do it properly, that I get an exaggerated amount of physical rest for the small time I spend, and I come out of it refreshed."

"It seems like a difficult technique."

"No, it's really very simple. There's no big ritual involved. You don't give up anything, just twenty minutes in the morning and twenty minutes in the evening. You find a comfortable spot to sit, close your eyes, fold your hands, allow your mind free range—and that's it."

He spreads his hands. "What you get out of it is a sense of euphoria. You feel good. It's a very, very pleasant procedure. It's as if something inside you begins to unwind the moment you start. Now I use it to relax during the business day, especially if I'm very tense. I sit down in my office chair, ask my secretary not to disturb me, turn off my desk lamp, and simply meditate.

"I find my whole body relaxing and I'm flooded with a deep, pleasurable feeling. The sense of relaxation is tremendous, as if someone were caressing me gently. I come out of it as relaxed as if I had taken a tranquilizer.

"You know, I've been to sessions where we meditated for four days off and on, and I've never had such pleasure. I've come out rested thoroughly and entirely. It's the most pleasant sensation I've ever felt."

He closes his eyes and assumes the lotus position again, leaving me to think over our discussion. Later that day I talk to my friend Bill, an advertising executive who has always lived on the brink of hysteria. Recently Bill has taken up transcendental meditation, but I know him for a hard-nosed realist.

"It's helped me," he confesses. "I enjoy it, and now I get more pleasure than I used to out of life. I don't know about the subtle states of thought that people talk about—I figure that's all gobbledygook. For my part meditation is really a pleasant experience. Hell, I paid sixty bucks to learn how!"

"What did you get for the money?"

"Instruction—and a mantra that's supposed to be mine alone. I don't share it with anyone. How does it work? I sit still and close my eyes and repeat the mantra over and over, concentrating on my breathing. Actually, the mantra is probably nonsense. I might just as well say one, one, one, over and over. What it does is keep you from thinking anxious and tense thoughts. Your breathing slows up and your body relaxes. It sort of recharges your batteries. Anyway, it works for me. Try it."

"Maybe I will. What's your mantra?"

"Ha! It may be nonsense, but it's mine. You want a mantra? Go buy your own for sixty bucks!"

The Politeness Game

"When I was a kid," Elliot tells me, "we used to play something we called the politeness game. The idea was to stop some man in the street and ask for the time, but to do it so politely and pleasantly that he gave you not only the time, but a smile and a few nice words as well."

"That was the game?"

"Well, we had a point system. One point for the time, a second for a smile, and a third for an answer, like 'That's all right'—or even 'You're welcome' when we said thank you. The fourth and most decisive point was awarded if he went on to ask our name or anything about us."

"But what was the idea of the game?"

"Well, on the surface the idea was just to rack up four points by being polite and cheery. But the truth was that I—and my friends too, I'm sure—got a tremendous charge out of being polite and seeing how that politeness forced a pleasant response."

"Did it always?"

"Almost always. Maybe because we were young and the part of town we lived in was rough, our politeness was unexpected. Most people were taken off guard—some were even a little upset, as if they were wondering, 'What's the kid after?'"

"But then, the funny thing was, a good many of the people held on to us."

"How do you mean, held on?"

"Well, they were reluctant to give us the time and walk away, to let it go at that. We were kind of a challenge, so pleasant and polite, and they were curious. The usual question was, 'Are you new here?' and I'd get a kick out of answering, 'Oh, no, sir. I've lived here all my life.' It shook them up. Most kids, to them, were mean little savages. Why were we so polite and mannerly?"

"Did you ever use the game later in life?"

"Well, usually not in that form, though from time to time I still stop people to ask the time and give them the full bit. It works, and it's fun to watch people's reaction.

"But when I was a teen-ager I used to play the game with the parents of the girls I went out with. I'd call the father sir, and I'd stand up when the mother came into the room."

"How did it work?"

Elliot laughs. "I'll tell you. The first time I tried it, the girl was furious. When we were alone, she said, 'Why are you making fun of my parents?' and I had a job convincing her I really meant it. But her parents—wow! From then on I could do no wrong. I was their fair-haired boy. They were furious with her, she told me, when we split up."

"But weren't you being hypocritical?"

"Yes and no. I enjoyed it tremendously. I get a great deal of pleasure out of pleasing someone else. I always thought of politeness as a little gift I could give someone, and I enjoyed the giving. I think most people enjoy giving gifts because they like to see others pleased.

"As for being hypocritical, I wasn't mocking anyone or pretending to be anything I wasn't. You see, there's a feedback to this game. In time politeness becomes a genuine part of your personality. Treating someone else with deference is normal for me now, and I still enjoy that little moment of surprise, that flush of pleasure when I give someone a seat in a crowded bus, or when I step back to let an older person get ahead of me."

I'm intrigued by Elliot's game, and when I tell it to a young friend he nods knowingly. "I can understand because I play the same game. I had a summer job at one of the quick-serve hamburger places, and I'd call the customers sir and thank them, and it's amazing what a response I got, especially, I'm convinced, since it was a poor neighborhood. It sounds corny, but I'd get a tremendous amount of pleasure out of seeing them walk out a little straighter."

Curiosity impelling me, I tried the politeness game myself. I began at the corner newsstand, where I'd always given and gotten a snarl with my morning paper. It worked! Not the first day, for ours was a long-term relationship, but on about the tenth day the newsdealer said, "Don't take the top paper. It's rumpled. Here, try from the middle of the pile."

It worked in other places too, to my own growing pleasure. I've come to realize how much of the little tensions of living are washed away by the politeness game.

I become doubly aware of it now when I run into someone else playing the same game. There's a momentary surprise, and then a quick smile of surrender. Neither of us is interested in one-upmanship. That's not the point of the game. The real victory is the glow of pleasure you get when someone else is moved by your politeness.

Running:
The Agony
and the Ecstasy

I have another half mile to go in my morning running around the local high school track and I can feel the sweat on my forehead and chest, the strain in my leg muscles, and the steady pounding of my heart. Don't think of the distance, just think of now, this section of track in front and behind you, breathe evenly and keep running. A quarter of a mile more, an eighth, and then—the end!

I slow down to a walk, breathing deeply, and my friend Morris, who runs with me, stops too. We both lean against the wall of the high school, supporting ourselves by our palms, and arch our backs into some tendon-stretching exercises.

Walking home, I ask Morris, "Do you really get any pleasure out of this?"

"Do you?"

I nod. "Yes. There's a wonderful glow of pleasure all through me right now, but I'm damned if I know why. I'm close to the edge of exhaustion."

He laughs. "I feel it too. I don't really know what the pleasure consists of. Sometimes I think it's that overwhelming exhaustion when you're convinced you can't go a step farther, yet you keep going—what accomplishment!

"Then sometimes I think it's nothing more than an over-whelming relief that it's all over, my poor tormented body can relax, and my racing heart can come back to normal!"

I shake my head. "I sometimes think all the pleasure comes afterward, when we get home all covered with sweat and get into a hot shower to steam away the sweat and the dirt and ease those aching, aching muscles!"

"Well," Morris chuckles. "Carry it a bit further. Maybe the real pleasure is sitting down to breakfast afterward, all dressed and showered, and telling your family, very casually, Oh, sure, I was up before the sun and I got my running in. Maybe that's what it's all about."

"Then why run?"

"How can you boast about having run if you don't? To tell the truth, I sometimes think that the pleasure of running is really a combination of all those things."

"But, you know," I say thoughtfully, "there is a kind of phys-ical exhaustion, when your heart races and you're all covered with sweat, that's painful in one sense, but wonderfully pleasant in another."

Morris nods. "It doesn't have to be running. I can get the same exhilaration from working out in a gym, not straining myself, using my body properly without taxing it, but still using it to the point of exhaustion. It's hard at first, but after a while you become aware of every muscle you have. It's a terribly intense and per-sonal awareness—and it's one of the greatest pleasures I know."

He stretches his arms. "Stopping and showering and relaxing afterward only frame it, showing you how your body has responded."

I agree. "I've gotten that same feeling with some sports—a good swift game of basketball, tennis, or anything else that calls for continuous exertion and body awareness."

"I used to go in for cross-country running when I was in high school," Morris recalls. "Somehow, being out there alone, covering the ground with no one to check you, intensified the feeling."

"The pleasure?"

"The pleasure and the pain. You wanted to give up and stop so badly you could taste it, and yet at the same time you were enjoying the strain, the terrible aching agony—and often it really was agony—of the running. I think," he says carefully, "that's really where the pleasure of running lies—in that peculiar juxtaposition of agony and ecstasy."

"Come on!"

"No, I'm serious. It is agony, and at the same time it's ecstasy. Sometimes I run and I get the feeling that this is what my body was made for, this is a normal state of living we've forgotten with civilization. Maybe man once hunted his prey by running after it. At any rate, I feel an ecstasy when I run, and sometimes I get the feeling that I could go on and on indefinitely."

We're at my house, and I wave goodbye and say, in parting, "With me it's mostly the shower and breakfast—and the relief that it's over."

The Images on My Mind

"My greatest pleasure," Sarah tells me, "comes from the images on my mind."

I watch her sitting in the easy chair in her neat, slightly overblown living room, a plump woman in her early seventies with gray hair that seems to be fighting a losing battle with hair-pins and nets.

"What do you mean?" I ask.

Smiling, she says, "I carry images with me of exquisite moments, images that are so vivid I can turn them on whenever I wish."

"I'm not sure I understand."

"Well, more than thirty years ago my husband and I were driving out West one autumn. I don't recall the state where I saw it, perhaps it was Idaho, but I do recall exactly what I saw. One isolated poplar tree, the only one in sight, and it had changed color. It was yellow, every leaf a glorious, brilliant yellow, and we saw it against a cloudless blue sky—such an intense blue. To this day I can close my eyes and see that yellow and blue—so vividly —and I get pleasure out of it!"

We're both silent for a moment, then I ask, "What other pleasures can you recall?"

"It is recall, and it's more than remembering. Those images exist. They are on my mind, brilliant on my mind. There's a mountain creek I remember from when I was a girl—just seventeen. It was the year World War I was over, and the boy I was in love with had come home. We drove up into the mountains in his father's flivver, and we parked and climbed down into this little gorge where the creek ran. There was a waterfall and a small pool. The water was cold but nice, and there were ferns and wild raspberry bushes all over the rocks.

"We both stripped!" She laughs. "Imagine swimming nude in 1919—and we swam there for an hour or more. The image I have is so terribly clear. It's of that boy—his naked body seemed so beautiful to me, climbing above the waterfall and diving into the pool and scrambling over the rocks. He had no sunburn, except on his face and neck. His skin was white and the pool threw a flickering reflected light over him and the rocks—I can see his body, the pink flowers of the wild raspberry, the green fern and the waterfall . . ."

She's silent, smiling softly, and then, before I can ask for another image, she says, "Another one that gives me so much pleasure is San Francisco. The first time I ever went there with my husband and he took me to the top of the Mark Hopkins Hotel. We had a drink and then looked down at the city. That view was really amazing, the white buildings, the sparkling green-blue of the bay, the red of the Golden Gate Bridge—there were dozens of white sailboats on the bay, like white birds. The city was so clean and crisp from up there.

"There's another city in one of my other images. It's not so nice, but it's real and alive."

"Which one is it?"

"New York. We went there one summer and we spent a week at one of the very nice hotels. It's funny, but I can't even remember the name of the hotel or where it was. In fact I can't remember much of that whole week. The weather was terribly hot and humid and the city seemed dirty and dreary, all concrete and brick—a terrible place to live.

"We took one sightseeing tour, and our bus went through Harlem. My image is from that trip. It's just the front of a house. I guess a tenement. It had fire escapes and there were people on all of them, sitting out on the ironwork fanning themselves. There were children on the front stoop of the house, but no one was talking and none of the children was playing. They were just sitting there, and they stared at our bus as we went by, not unkindly, but not even curiously—they just stared, and I felt utterly sad."

She sighs. "That image is New York to me. It always will be, and still, in some unhappy way, I find it pleasant to recall it."

Again we're quiet, then she says brightly, "But there are hundreds of other images that aren't at all sad. There's my bagpiper."

"Who was he?"

"I don't know. It was more than forty years ago and we took our children camping. We were living near Boston then, and we drove up the coast to Maine and camped at Mount Desert Island. I remember one morning Barney and I took a walk alone and I began gathering wildflowers—there were thousands. We heard this lovely, keening noise, and Barney said, 'My God, it's a bagpiper!'

"We rounded a big, rocky hill and there—it's one of the clearest images I have—on the crest of the hill was a young man with bright red hair and kilts and a bagpipe. I'll always treasure that early-morning moment of seeing the bagpipe player on the hill of wildflowers."

"Why was he playing in such a remote place?" I ask, fascinated.

She shakes her head. "We never found out. We didn't want to disturb him. We just listened for a long time, and then wandered off—our morning too perfect to spoil it with explanations."

Moving the Ball Along

I talk to Brian, an English student, on the bench after the soccer game while a group of children kick the ball around the field. Brian played well and now, breathless and sweating, he sits in his striped jersey and shorts and stretches out his well-muscled legs.

"What I like about soccer," he tells me, "is that it's such a mixture of individual and teamwork. When you're playing you can be very good by yourself—you know, show off as much as you like, but you can also play as part of the team. You just have to work with your teammates to put that ball into the goal.

"Then, too, it's not a rigid game—it's far from your football, with all its diagrammed plays and line-ups. There's a lot more flair to soccer. You see, there's a lot of skill involved in playing it, but even people without much skill—people of any age—can play."

"Isn't that a contradiction?"

"Not really. It depends on whether you're playing competitively, to win, or just for fun. You need a bloody lot of skill in a competitive game, certainly, but if the pleasure you get is just in the playing—why, anyone can kick a ball around, and that's fun!

"There's a wonderful, exultant kind of pleasure in moving a ball across the field. During a game, when you're trying to get into position to score and keep the other team from capturing the ball, it's one kind of pleasure, but I've had great times all by myself on an empty soccer field just moving the ball along.

"In a game, one of the great pleasures is recognizing where other people will be at any given moment and passing the ball to just that spot, even before they get there. If you hit it just right—well! You feel so good!

"When I play defense, of course it isn't as much fun as when I score. The ultimate pleasure of soccer is scoring a goal. When you shoot that ball hard and hear the zing as it goes into the net, you feel an exhilaration that I can't even begin to describe.

"And of course there's the physical part of it all. During a game you have to work furiously. You know, a soccer game is ninety bloody minutes long with only one ten-minute intermission. You're constantly running and it's very strenuous—but pleasantly so. I love that feeling and the shower afterward. You have a sense of accomplishment then—you've actually done something.

"I also get an enormous amount of pleasure out of watching soccer. When I see someone as great as, say, Pelé, I get an incredible feeling. I really begin to believe that I can do what he's doing. And I can, of course—the only difference is that he can do it a hundred times as well!

"Another delightful source of pleasure in the game is the gracefulness I sense in my own motions when I'm playing well. I twist and turn perfectly. You know, soccer is a very fast game. When you get the ball you have to move quickly and make your mind up in a matter of seconds about what you're going to do —and do it.

"There's another funny thing about the game, though, that may be peculiar to England."

"What's that?" I ask.

Brian looks at the shouting children kicking the ball and he smiles. "Well, it's the crowd hysteria you feel as an onlooker. I've watched games and felt it myself. It's a different sort of pleasure, but it's a pleasure to give yourself up to that hysteria."

"Identifying with the crowd?"

"And feeling that they feel. The crowd gets fantastically excited and you feel a tremendous emotional release with everybody screaming. When one of your favorite players scores a goal, you just go mad. I can't explain why, but it's definitely a part of the fun.

"Maybe for us players it's a kind of identification. If you've played the game, you can become so involved with the match you're watching that you become a part of it. You share all the player's emotions—but sharpened and pointed up. And if you're in that mood and your team wins—well, then you're in heaven."

He stops talking and jumps up suddenly as the kids' ball comes bouncing toward our bench. "Hey! I'll be back in a minute!" and he moves the ball gracefully across the field to the waiting kids.

Creative Cookery

"I used to shop in a little fish store across town," Vera tells me, "and for its size it was remarkable. It carried just about every type of fish you could imagine—and every type of customer. I enjoyed talking to the other people who shopped there, people of all different nationalities, and getting their recipes. Sometimes I gave them mine.

"Once the fish store carried fresh herring, and one of the men who came from Holland asked me if I'd ever eaten it raw. I was fascinated and he told me how to prepare it the way they do in Amsterdam, skinned with oil and onion and vinegar. It was just wonderful, and my family raved about it. That's the real pleasure I get out of cooking."

"Your family's approval?"

"Oh, that's part of it, sure. I love to make something that

excites them. I love the fact that when I call my friends and invite them for supper they'll break any date to come. I guess it's a kind of ego trip for me, doing something well, but really the pleasure is more than that.

"I think most of my fun comes from the act of cooking. I taste constantly when I cook, and I get a kick out of balancing the spices to make the flavor just right—but I feel that there's a creative art to cooking, and that's what turns me on."

"Isn't everything spelled out by the recipe?"

"I never really follow a recipe that closely. I can usually tell, just by reading it, whether it's going to be good or not, or what I'll have to change to make it better. I guess it's half intuition and half experience, but I always take something away and add something else, and inevitably I come up with something a little better than the original. That gives me a real creative pleasure.

"But, truthfully, I suppose a big part of the pleasure is my audience's reaction. I couldn't cook just for myself. When I'm alone I always prepare things that can be used as leftovers, so in effect I'm still cooking for my family.

"Then, too, I take a great pride in turning out something different, even if I haven't made it up myself. Like my baked mussels. My friends and family consider it my specialty, but actually I got the recipe from a man in that same fish store, a Frenchman.

"I was buying mussels and he started telling me about them, how to tell which are good—with a charming French accent—and then he said, 'I hope you're not going to steam them in white wine,' which was just what I was going to do.

"I said, 'Why not?' and he shrugged. 'Everyone steams them in white wine. You want something superb? Steam them just a bit to open them, then put them on the half shell and add some melted butter with parsley in it and fresh garlic and top it with grated Parmesan cheese and bake it. *Voilà!*'

"I tried it, and though I never saw that man again, I'm eternally grateful for the pleasure his recipe has given me. You see, that's one of the real pleasures of cooking—finding a recipe that isn't in a cookbook, or at least that you haven't seen in a cookbook, and pleasing someone else with it."

"Then a good part of the pleasure is the audience?"

"No artist can survive without an audience," she says simply. "Sure, the audience reaction is tremendously important for your pleasure, but so is the creative aspect. Even if my family loved steak, I'd get no kick out of preparing steak each night. There's also the exploratory aspect."

"What's that?"

"Well—let's see how I can explain it. It's such an important part of cooking—like trying something new, or making do with something you have. Up in the country I wanted to make a sorrel soup, but it was past the season for good sour sorrel, and my husband came home with a mess of purslane he'd found in a nearby stream. Well, I used the same recipe and ended up with a delicious purslane soup. Purslane is a wild watercress. The soup tasted different, but the family flipped over it.

"We spent one summer down in Mexico and did our own cooking. We had to make do with what was available: hundreds of limes, fresh marjoram—which incidentally tasted fabulous—wild mint, and the most wonderful pork. Also the wrong altitude and a gas stove that was slow. I'd bake the pork for hours with marjoram and baste it with lime juice. I had to bake it slowly because of the oven, but the result was sensational!

"When I face a handicap and turn it into a virtue, cooking really gives me pleasure."

"Are you an organized cook?"

She looks askance. "Lord, no. My kitchen is terribly disorganized. Oh, I know where everything is, but I spread myself all over. I'm very possessive about my kitchen. I resent anyone else doing the actual cooking, but I love having people help with the dirty work—the peeling and chopping and preparation—the tedious stuff. The only reason I'm patient enough to do it is because it's the only way to enjoy the pleasure of cooking."

She hesitates a moment. "It's hard to pinpoint the exact pleasure I get out of cooking, though I do get a tremendous amount. Maybe it's a sense of control, of power. Food is such a basic thing, isn't it? We all need it to survive. If I'm a good or a great cook, it puts the power of survival in my hands. That kind of control is exciting—and I suppose there's a nurturing element too. I like to cook for my own family or close friends more than for anyone else.

"Another thing that gives me a real kick is duplicating dishes. If I have a delicious dish somewhere I never ask for the recipe. It's a matter of pride to me to see if, by experiment, I can duplicate that dish exactly. Sometimes I'll not only duplicate it, but I'll actually improve it and that's the best of all.

"I tasted a Chinese chicken dish once that I thought was heavenly. I fooled around and found that if I took chicken breasts and marinated them with soy sauce, garlic, ginger root, oil and sherry wine and added sesame seeds, lemon, and a touch of apricot jam and baked them I ended up with something much better than the original. That accomplishment and the approval of my family—they're the real joys of cooking!"

The Psychosomatic Bath

Meg and Barry have just finished their summer home, and they show me through it proudly. It's rustic in a very nice way, and I compliment them on its modest design—until we get to the bathroom. There I am absolutely speechless.

I face an ordinary set of appliances, a built-in shower, and a most extraordinary tub. This is no porcelain or fiberglass product, but is built out of tile, sunk below the floor level three feet deep, and it measures eight feet by eight.

On one side of the tub from floor to ceiling is an enormous picture window with a view of trees and distant mountains. There are dozens of potted plants along the window sill, almost creating the illusion of a wooded pool.

"How do you like it?" Meg asks.

Overwhelmed, I say, "I don't know which is greater, the tub or the view."

"We think it's a fabulous combination. It's big enough for the whole family."

After dinner Meg talks to me seriously about her views on baths. "I get so much pleasure out of taking a bath, not in the old sense of scrubbing myself clean in the tub, but more in the Japanese manner. Barry and I spent five years in Japan after the war."

"What do you mean about the Japanese manner?"

"Well, we don't bathe to get clean. In Japan they have little faucets near the tub with stools to sit on. You sit down and scrub up there and rinse clean with a bucket of water before you get into the tub, and that's what we do.

"We take a very quick shower, soap up, and rinse off. In the meantime we fill the tub with hot water and add a scented bath powder. There's one that turns the water a sort of iridescent green and has a very gentle odor. Then we slip into the tub and just soak. Usually Barry and I take a bath together, but sometimes the children join us and we've even had guests take a tub with us."

"Without clothes?"

Meg looks at me in amusement. "If anyone wants to wear clothes they can—if the clothes are clean."

Feeling silly, I say, "It's just that I'm not used to the idea."

"Of course not, but if you consider it for a minute, you'll see how silly it is to be hung up about nudity. It's not a sexual experience, tubbing. It's a sensual experience and a spiritual one. That's why we have the plants near the window and why we faced the window toward the mountains and trees."

"I don't quite see how it's spiritual."

"Perhaps it's the word *spiritual*. I don't mean it in any supernatural sense. I might just as well have said *psychological*. I feel that the absolute relaxation you can obtain in a tub—the physical relaxation, the warmth of the water calming your muscles—also puts you into a relaxed psychological or spiritual state. You can eliminate the anxieties and tensions of day-to-day living, all the petty little annoyances, and you can free your mind to concentrate on spiritual beauty."

"Such as?"

"Well, the mountains beyond the window, the trees and the

sky, the clouds—the beauty and calm of nature. And if you're not fortunate enough to build a tub with a view, you can do what we've done. We've brought a small part of nature into the bathroom itself with the plants on the window sill. You can sit and soak and trace the edge of a leaf or the beauty of a flower, the bending of a stem—all that is beauty!"

"But is beauty only in nature?"

"Of course not. Man can create beauty. I have friends whose bathrooms have ordinary tubs, but they were able to create a serene and pleasant environment in the room with paint or pictures or screens or even wallpaper—anything to give a sense of beauty that you can dwell on. Then tubbing becomes more than a way of getting clean or relaxing your body. It becomes a way of relaxing your mind too, an exquisitely pleasurable experience."

"She's right, you know," Barry agrees, laughing. "We have that kind of bathroom in our city apartment and its tub is an ordinary one, but the room is fixed up beautifully. I can come home from the worst day at the office, take a quick shower to clean off, and then soak in a luxurious tub for ten or fifteen minutes and come out refreshed in my body and spirit—or psyche if that's better."

"And of course there's the water itself," Meg adds. "There are the things you can put into it, the bubble baths and different scents, the water softeners and bath oils—they all create an environment that soothes you on every level.

"What you must learn," she stresses, "in order to bathe properly is the entire ritual involved—washing beforehand, the proper filling of the tub, the ability to cleanse your mind as well as your body, and the ability to concentrate on beauty. I have a friend who uses roses when she bathes. She takes two or three perfect ones and floats them on the water."

"Doesn't the heat kill them?"

"Eventually, yes, but for the length of her bath they remain open and perfect. She relaxes in the tub and studies the shape of each flower, the turn of each petal and its color, and she lets her mind probe and understand the flower while her body is soothed by the warmth of the water."

Barry nods. "And I have a friend who bathes in near-darkness. He has a subdued light with a turning wheel in front of it that sends flickering shadows over the water and his body."

"Whatever you use," Meg assures me, "the point is that it becomes not only a pleasant physical experience, but an emotional one as well. The body and the mind are really one, you know."

"What you advocate is a psychosomatic bath."

"Exactly. And now, if you'd like to, we can all tub together."

Traveling by Thumb

"You have to like people to get pleasure out of hitchhiking," Bob tells me. "More than like, you have to enjoy every type of person from the perverted to the straight."

"I always looked on hitchhiking as a way of getting from here to there," I say.

"It can be, but to me it's always been much more. I get the greatest pleasure out of taking a few days and getting out on the road and hitching. I don't care where I go or if I get anywhere. The pleasure I get is in meeting different people and experiencing different surroundings."

"What do you mean by surroundings?"

"Well, sometimes I'll be stuck by the side of the road for an hour or more. When that happens you can go two routes—the anxiety way, where you get all uptight thinking, When will I get my next hitch, will I be here all day, why doesn't anyone stop?

"Or you can go the relaxed route. Here I am by the side of the road where the grass is growing, the flowers are blooming, the sun is out, it's a lovely day. What more can I want? I'll enjoy this piece of now. Then I look around me and see things from a new perspective, from ground level. I really look at insects and flowers, at trees, at the frog in the culvert, or the rabbit in the patch of blackberry bushes—there's an entire small world in any one spot on the road.

"If it's raining, I enjoy the rain. I see it as something to water the plants. I watch the drops falling and try to see the beauty in them, the romance behind them, the water lifted from lakes and oceans and carried by the clouds and wind."

"All that by the side of the road?"

"And much more! Inevitably a lift comes, and if you really dig that spot by the side of the road, the lift always comes too soon. But the compensation is that by taking the lift you're going to experience another pleasure of hitching—meeting people.

"You know, I'm really a small-town boy, and hitching has given me a chance to meet all kinds of people all over America —and, I guess, to realize what America is really like. To me, it's always a challenge to see if I can communicate with other people.

"You can talk, sure, that's easy, but really communicating is a different thing. You have to see what both of you have in common—and if you look hard enough you always see something.

"Once I was hitching from Indiana to Kentucky, and a real racist guy picked me up. We couldn't have been further apart in our thinking. Well, I rode with him for six hours, and we did have something in common—we were both country-music freaks. At the end of the ride, neither of us had changed, but I think we each learned something. I know I learned that I had my own prejudices, and as for him—well, I've got a beard and maybe he learned that bearded men aren't all weirdos.

"I find it amazing, when I hitchhike, how many people who pick me up are stoned on one thing or another and try to get me to try their stuff. Dozens of people have offered me reefers, and truck drivers have pushed bennies on me. Once I got a hitch with a very straight young couple who had a case of beer in the back seat. They kept drinking and throwing the empties out the window and urging me to join them. I had the feeling that something was terribly wrong between them, but I never found out what it was. It was a far-out ride!"

"Did you really enjoy it?"

"Well, I found it fascinating. It's been on my mind a lot since then. What was troubling those two? They looked so straight, such establishment types—I guess guys like me tend to think establishment types never have any problems. But it was the type of human contradiction I enjoy when I find it.

"Still, most people are pretty normal, and most want to talk. That's what gives me the most pleasure, finding out what people do, how they live, how different they are—and still how much they're like you.

"The surprising thing, you find out, is that most people are nice. I've been taken into homes for the night by perfect strangers who picked me up, fed me, and even offered me money when they thought I was broke. Hell, I'm just brushing thirty, yet women have asked me if my folks know where I am and have offered to call them and tell them I'm all right! It's nice to know people still care.

"Oh, there are some people who'll pick you up and then not talk at all. Others just ask questions, and some will tell you everything, what they do for a living, where they live—even their most intimate problems. I guess they feel comfortable because they're sure they'll never see you again.

"Once I was picked up by a blacksmith, a real honest-to-goodness blacksmith in this day and age. Yeah, there's a lot of pleasure in hitching, provided you don't have to get anywhere.

"And, you know, you see differently when you hitch. For one thing, the roads are smaller because you tend to travel the back ways, and sometimes it's very beautiful there. You can forget how beautiful the country can be when you're whizzing by on a superhighway. In hitching you travel by fits and starts, and I get pleasure out of that."

Remembering Bob's words, I stopped to pick up a hitchhiker a few weeks later. He was a young man on his way home from work, a bright articulate fellow who turned a boring trip into a pleasant ride that was over too soon. After that I began to look for hitchhikers whenever I drove alone, and I've explored the pleasure of hitching from the driver's side.

Of course, it's not all sunshine and roses. I've picked up some surly people, and one or two who made me realize there is a danger involved. You take a chance with every hitchhiker you pick up—but pleasure often involves taking chances.

Between Sex and Opera

"If I had to rate the pleasure of fireworks on a scale," Chris tells me, "I'd put it somewhere between sex and opera."

"Is it like music?"

"Almost, but it's visual as well as auditory. To me, the most thrilling part of a good fireworks display is the color against the black sky. That and the noise! The explosion of sound and color and light all at once really sends me. It's a completely emotional experience."

He thinks for a moment, then nods. "You know, I get the biggest thrill out of the kind of fireworks that shoot up into the sky. Seeing them, hearing them—it's almost orgiastic for me, and it fills me with joy and hilarity. I want to laugh and shout and yell.

"When it's over, I feel emotionally drained, but in a very good sense. I'm satiated, washed out—if it's been a good display."

"What is the best display you've seen?"

Chris's eyes sparkle. "The most fantastic fireworks I've ever seen were Japanese, but then the very best fireworks are always Japanese. This was back in 1957, when I was just a kid. There was a big Japanese trade fair that year—it was just becoming respectable to like the Japanese again. Their government sent over an official fireworks display, and they had three barges out in the river. There were a lot of set pieces—you know, a gigantic Niagara Falls in the middle flanked by portraits of their emperor and our president. I don't go for that type of display myself. It's too contrived, too rigid and set, but the climax of the show, wow! I still remember that.

"It was five minutes of something they called flowering chrysanthemums. It started low, almost at barge level, streaks of green stems and leaves and small buds and flowers, and then it just seemed to explode higher and higher, a fantastic, dazzling display of yellow, orange, and red chrysanthemums in the sky, huge flowers erupting and fading and erupting again with a finale of rocket after rocket, and then each would fade away to nothing.

"That fading away, that terribly ephemeral quality of fireworks, really grabs me. It's an experience in time without reference to anything you can look at concretely. Even a photograph can't capture it because it's a progression and the total impact has to hit you. Perhaps a motion picture could do it."

Ann, Chris's wife, has been listening, and now she shakes her head. "To me the real pleasure of fireworks is the rockets. Oh, the rest is fun to watch, and I do get a charge out of it, but nothing compares to the way I feel when a rocket goes off. I'm not like Chris. I don't want to shout. I'm too tight, too keyed up to shout. I gasp, no matter how often I see it, and then I get such a feeling of sadness, of longing—I can feel the tears come to my eyes. I follow that rocket up, up, up—the higher it goes the tighter I feel, and then when it bursts, it's as if a steel band across my chest snapped open."

Chris looks at her in surprise. "But is that pleasant?"

"Oh, yes! You've no idea what a sense of freedom it gives me, of exaltation and—breathlessness. It is pleasure, the most exciting kind of pleasure!"

"But only the rockets? I go crazy when the Roman candles go off. They have to be the most."

"What about the ones that burst into a shower of colored stars and then each star bursts again into another shower?" I ask. "I like those the best, and they last the longest."

Ann disagrees. "They haven't the splendor of the rockets—nor the sound, and that final wild explosion way, way up!"

"I'm not sure that the noise really sends me," I protest. "It's the visual display that I enjoy, and there's something else. Fireworks remind me of my childhood. My father always used to take us out to one of the beaches on the Fourth of July, and we'd watch the local fire department set off a display over the water. I don't remember much noise, but I do remember the crowd going *Oh!* and *Ah!* as each display flared up and died, and at the really good ones everybody'd clap."

Chris shakes his head. "There has to be noise for me, and that great fountain of erupting light."

Ann smiles. "I still love the rockets. Someday, Chris, I want to get down to Cape Kennedy when they send a real one up. Now that would be pleasure!"

The Nose Knows

Miriam has just opened a small scent shop in town, and the entire street is fragrant with her runaway odors.

"You know, I like to think of my shop as a way-out nose trip," Miriam tells me. "We all love smells. It's just something born into us. Even dogs. You let them run in the woods and they'll find some dead, ripe animal and roll around in it till they smell to high heaven, and then come back pleased as punch with themselves.

"Myself, I love smells. I love soft things like lotions and bubble baths, and I'm always trying out new scents on myself. One day I'll walk into a room with a fresh lilac scent, and I'll see people looking around puzzled. Lilacs? At this time of year? Oh, wow! I love that."

"When did you get into smells?"

She shrugs and brushes her dark hair back. "I don't know. I think I've always been turned on by smells, and I love to turn other people on to them too. I think it's beautiful when some burly masculine type comes in and I spray a little love oil on him and tell him to taste it—"

"Taste it?"

"Oh, sure. Don't you know what love oil is?"

"No, I don't think I've ever seen it."

"Well, it's a lotion with a glycerine base and a few other ingredients. It gets warm when you blow on it, and it's edible too. We flavor it with chocolate or strawberry or cherry vanilla and add a little food coloring. It's way out when you use it to make love. You see, it gives a new pleasure to the whole thing, odor."

"And taste?"

"Exactly. That's far out. You know, smelling is very close to taste. You stimulate both and you have a—what's the word?—a synergistic experience.

"But, you know, everyone has a scent that's just right for him or her. It's like their astrological sign. I think it's a real challenge to find a person's perfect scent, like casting a horoscope for them. Some people just don't understand their own character, and sometimes a fragile little woman will come in wanting a strong, aggressive scent. I try and steer her to the right one."

"How do you cast the right horoscope?"

"Odorscope," she corrects me, and she gestures vaguely. "Part of it is just intuition. I look at a person and something tells me what they should smell like. I have dozens of different odors and I can blend hundreds of combinations. I blend by feel, and then I take their character and personality into account. I talk to them first to find out what they're like.

"You know, Billie Holiday's odorscope was gardenias. That was her flower and her scent. Well, everyone is like that—or should be. Each person should have one special scent."

"Do you?"

"No. I like to change my scent. There are just too many different ones for me to ever settle on one. Each scent gives me a different pleasure, opens my head to a different trip. I can close my eyes and find a whole new dimension of smell."

"Don't all these odors deaden your sense of smell?"

"No. If anything, they sharpen it. You know, over and above the artificial odors everyone has an odor of their own, and I'm into those natural odors too. I like to smell a person's natural odor."

"You mean body odor?"

"Yes, but that's become such a bad term because of all the advertising campaigns against it. Actually, body odors are nice, quiet, and subtle, like identifying keys to a person. It's only when sweat gets into your clothes and turns sour that odor becomes offensive. The odor of a body right after a shower or a bath is very pleasant, and unique for each person. What I like to do is match and complement that odor and emphasize it with a scent."

She wrinkles her nose charmingly and smiles. "I'll tell you, things are going back to a more formal life-style. It used to be that everyone was into sloppy clothes and messed-up hair and rank odors—the funky look. Now we're beginning to be very conscious of how we dress and how we style our hair—men and women—and the rank smell is out. People want sophisticated, subtle odors.

"They're becoming aware of scented shampoos and creme rinses, soaps and sachets—that's the big, new thing in smell, sachet. I mix them from bowls of dried blossoms and herbs." She waves to a table filled with dozens of jars of flower petals and dried leaves. "I make them for drawers and closets, sure, but I also mix them for cars and houses, for kitchens and bathrooms.

"You know, I don't really sell my scents," she says confidentially, blending a few petals to show me. "I simply turn people on to smells and let them take it from there."

I end up taking a sachet for my pocket, and I walk home pleasantly aware of the very subtle flower odor. It wouldn't be at all bad to have a house smell like this, or an office, I think, smiling in spite of myself.

Sailing Free

"The happiest summer of my life," Irv told me, "was the summer of '70. It was the first year we bought a sailboat that we could cruise in. It slept four, but our whole family set out on a real trip—my wife, myself, our four kids, and the dog. The older kids slept on deck. That trip gave all of us a sense of accomplishment, because each of us had a job and we all worked together.

"We had all kinds of days, but the one I remember best was coming into Mystic Harbor. We had to pass the Race, a swift current over a deep and uneven bottom. The water boils as it runs against the wind.

"It was a brisk summer day and we came across heeled over, literally bouncing from one wave to another. Everyone was topside. That was a passage we all remember! There was such a feeling of triumph when we finally made it across the Race, came bearing down on the drawbridge and signaled it with four toots of our horn, then yelled with delight as it actually opened for our little ship.

"To this day all of us remember the beauty of that approach, the family together and the boat a part of the family. That was pleasure!"

I asked Irv if he considered himself a sailing freak.

"Sailing for pleasure never occurs to me," he said thoughtfully, "but, of course, I do get pleasure out of it—that's why I do it. It's even more than pleasure. Every aspect of sailing pleases me—yet it's not relaxation."

Pressed, he explained, "Relaxation is letting go and doing nothing. Sailing is the other side of the coin. You're always doing something, at sea or ashore. I'm always totally involved with my boat, and I love every aspect of it, sanding the bottom, tuning the motor, getting the mast and sails in shape—it's all backbreaking work. Funny, I hate cleaning my house, but I love polishing my boat. Maybe it's pride of ownership, the power principle.

"Apart from maintenance, while you're sailing the boat you're constantly keyed up, involved with managing the sails, aware of every change in the direction of the wind and waiting to adjust the sails accordingly. You're always alert, conscious of the weather, the wind, the sky—you're ready for any emergency, and when one comes up you have to summon all your coping skills at a second's notice.

"To me," he continued, "the sailboat is one of the most efficient, beautiful, and effective machines man has ever devised. It's absolutely functional, and that's where its beauty lies."

"But what do you feel?" I asked, puzzled. "Where does the pleasure come from?"

"In the liberating, free act of sailing. In the knowledge that you're in control of this hurtling monster. The top speed of my boat is six knots—about seven and a half miles an hour—but from the deck that speed is like flying.

"Then there's the ever present sense of danger to heighten your enjoyment. I love getting up early in the morning while we're at anchor to find a pea-soup fog all around us. Getting out of a complicated harbor with that white stuff packed solid all over gives me a terrific sense of accomplishment. I feel a master, not only over the boat, but over the elements. I feel excitement and adventure, pride and elation.

"And sailing offers so many different experiences. Sometimes you race along briskly on a beautiful day with a ten-to-fifteen-knot breeze, and there's an exultant sense of uplift you get from nothing else.

"Some passages are sheer drudgery, with too much wind and a following sea. They are pure work, but there is pleasure in accomplishment, in beating the elements."

Considering a moment, he said, "I love the clear, breezy days, but I also love the leaden skies with the sea like slate, and ominous days with a strong wind. I love bundling up against the cold, wearing sweaters to keep warm. There's a gray beauty then that equals the hot days when we can strip down in the sparkling sun."

"How would I start sailing? What kind of boat would I buy?"

"I'd find a good friend first and sail with him. Don't rush out to buy a boat. There are sailing schools that will teach you the basics in a week or two. When you feel that you're ready to buy, buy a little more than you can afford, a size bigger than you think you'll need. I can guarantee that the day after your first sail you'll need a bigger boat."

He smiled at me. "Remember, Allah does not deduct from the allotted hours of man the time spent sailing."

Listening for Pleasure

Walking through the woods, Milt and I come on a young man with a rifle out hunting. I say hello and he answers with a rather rude remark about strangers. I walk away, annoyed, but Milt lingers, talking to the young man in spite of his rudeness. Soon I see that the hostility is gone and they're deep in conversation.

Later Milt joins me. "He was very interesting, that guy. He knows all the best spots for small game around here."

"I felt he was rude."

"Well—" Milt brushes that aside. "Maybe he thought we'd give him a hard time for hunting here, but I had a nice talk with him, I learned a lot."

I realize that Milt always has a nice talk, no matter how unyielding the other person seems at the beginning. When I ask him about it, he says, "Well, I get a tremendous pleasure out of listening to all kinds of people."

"Talking with them?"

"No, listening. You know, almost everyone has something worth listening to. Take old Hollenbeck."

"Who's he?"

"Well, he runs a sawmill over in the next valley. He's almost ninety years old, but still strong as an ox. He runs the mill himself and still does a full day's work, but you listen to him talk and it's fascinating. Most people dismiss him as a little senile because of his age, but he isn't. He has all his marbles, and it's amazing how much he's picked up over the years. Anything you want to know about lumber, or about this area, he knows it—and a lot more. He was a whiskey runner during Prohibition, and he'll tell you stories about those days and even about the 1800's. Imagine that!

"I never get bored listening to someone like that. I go in to buy some wood and he'll tell me, No, get this instead, and then he explains why and he's right.

"You know, when you listen to other people talking it takes you out of your own head. I have a friend who goes in for mountain climbing, and when I start him off he can talk about it for hours. I not only learn a lot, but I get a vicarious pleasure out of his experiences.

"There's so much knowledge locked up in other people, and very few of us make the most of it. All you need is the right key to unlock it. Me, I like to listen if there's something on the other end. I've talked to truck drivers and pilots, counter men and motorcyclists and God knows who else. Sometimes it's boring, but usually it's interesting and you can learn something. If you want the real pleasure of listening, you have to forget about your own ego, making your own point, telling your own stories. You have to listen and be genuinely interested—and draw the other person out."

I think about Milt's words, and I recall that my young friend Alison is also intrigued with listening to other people.

"Mostly," she says, "I like to listen to older people. Many of them have fascinating backgrounds, and if you let them see you're interested they'll open up and tell you all kinds of things. It's like a personal history lesson.

"My own grandmother, for instance. You know, I just found out that she came across America in a covered wagon when she was a baby. Her father took the whole family West, and they had a terrible time crossing the prairie. Her mother died, but her father kept going with the children. It's a fantastic story, and no one in the family knew it until I took the time to listen to her.

"My father's parents also have an interesting story. His father was drafted into the Tsar's army, and he escaped by pretending to be drowned. He left his uniform on the bank of the river and swam downstream, where some friends were waiting with clothes, and they smuggled him out of Russia! He has so many wild stories of his adventures before he got here. I believe them all, and I have such fun listening to them.

"And there are Dad's cousins who escaped from Nazi Germany. One of them was the only Jewish girl left in a German village, and the villagers hid her every night in a different barn—I tell you, the stories those people tell if you can get them to open up!"

"How do you do it?"

"Well, first you have to convince them that you want to listen. You'd be surprised how many people don't. Most people only want to talk, to tell their story or get their ideas out. Listening is another matter. I think it's really a rare skill."

"How do you develop it?"

"You have to be prepared for boredom, because for every fascinating story there are a dozen dull ones, but still, even the dullest story has some intriguing elements in it.

"There's another aspect of listening that I get a great kick out of." She lowers her voice, though we're alone. "That's eaves-dropping."

"Really?"

"Oh, yes. I do it all the time. It's sort of a vice with me, but it doesn't hurt anyone. You can hear the most wonderful snatches of reality, little snippets of other people's lives floating through partitions or from neighboring bus seats. The only trouble is, I always want to interrupt and ask, What happened then? What did he do? What did she mean?

"It's funny, but when you really begin to listen you find that even the most ordinary, seemingly dreary lives have flashes of brilliance. Eavesdropping, like listening, gives you a glimpse of all of that."

Two from Column A

"I never knew how really fabulous eating out could be," José says, "until our trip to Europe five years ago."

"Where did you go?"

"The question is, how did we go. My wife came into a very small inheritance, two thousand dollars, and we decided to blow it all on a transatlantic cruise. We went first class on the *France*."

"Was it worth it?"

"For the food alone! I have never eaten as well as I did in that dining room. To begin with, the service was perfect. The waiters were efficient, and yet they gave you the idea that you really counted. They wanted to take care of you. When they served a fish it was a treat to see them bone it at the serving cart. When they carved, it was masterfully done. We had pheasant once, and the way they cut it and served it was a treat in itself.

"The tables were set exquisitely, and of course the dining room was beautifully decorated. We dressed for dinner almost every night, the men in black and white evening clothes and the women in beautiful gowns—such an elegant touch. Even if the food were ordinary, the setting would have been remarkable.

"But the food was far from ordinary. I've honestly never tasted such fine cooking, even the rolls and salads—that salad dressing! I asked the waiter and he said it was just some dry mustard in oil with a little vinegar—but we could never duplicate it at home.

"The meat and fish were always perfect, and always served with incredible sauces. That crossing was five days of exquisite pleasure. What a shame they've taken the *France* out of service—not that I could ever afford to go again."

"Sometimes," I tell José, "I think that eating out is a three-part thing. First there's the ambience, the decoration of the restaurant. I've been to some remarkable places, one that had a huge fireplace in the middle of the room, like an inverted funnel, with a crackling fire going, and another place on top of a tall building with two glass walls that looked down on the entire city. The view was breathtaking, especially at dusk when the lights began to come on in the buildings.

"Then there are the quaint places, and they can give me almost as much pleasure—the little hole-in-the-wall type with checked tablecloths and candles in wine bottles. Sometimes they're too precious to be true, but occasionally you hit one that's a natural. You just know there's no fakery involved. I went to one like that once in Provincetown on the wharf—oh, years ago. It didn't have any of the fake fishnet decor, but it had nice weathered wood walls, scrubbed oak tables, and candles in hurricane lamps on each table—but it was all real, and so was the food."

José nods. "The best ambience I ever found was in a tiny vest-pocket-sized place in Minneapolis. Would you believe it, there were only four tables, but I never saw one empty. It was a family enterprise, where Papa cooked while Mama managed and their son waited on tables. That room was so clean you could have literally eaten off the floor. There were a few very good oil paintings on the walls, and each table had matched linen and dishes. Eating there was a visual treat as well as a gustatory one."

"On the visual level, I'm turned on by the Italian restaurants that display tables of cold hors d'oeuvre—those marvelous stuffed artichokes and cold mussels, green and black with the red of pimento—"

"As for ambience," José interrupts, "I remember a restaurant in Paris, on one of those islands in the river, which must still be the way it was in medieval times, with great bowls of raw vegetables for a salad course and tremendous bowls of sausages and cheese for a first course."

"The second pleasure in eating out," I decide, "is the service. There is nothing nicer or more soothing to the ego than the kind of nurturing you get with good restaurant service. I don't mean obsequious service. I mean competent, thoughtful, polite service, when the waiter treats you as a guest and you treat him as a human being. There's nothing as distasteful as a rude guest in a restaurant."

José agrees. "Guest is the key word. When you're treated as a guest instead of a customer, you can't help but take pleasure in eating out."

"The third thing, of course, is the food."

Again José nods. "I don't think any pleasure can quite match that of eating exceptionally good food. Myself, I've tried most and I find that French cooking is on top of my list. French chefs are really creative artists in the kitchen. And you know, growing up in America, it never hit me that French fries were a French dish, until I went to a French restaurant in Washington and found they served only steak and French fries. At first I was disappointed at the limited menu—but when I tasted those potatoes, it was like a light illuminating the darkness!"

I laugh. "I do like French cooking, but to me the most creative, the tastiest and most imaginative, is the Chinese type. What they can do with a whole sea bass is remarkable, and dishes like mu shu pork or lemon chicken or Szechuan beef and watercress— that's cooking and eating.

"My only complaint about good Chinese food is that so many restaurants bring all the dishes together. They should bring one at a time, so you can savor the pleasure of each. Of course, in a busy restaurant, there's a problem of logistics."

"You mustn't overlook Japanese food," José puts in. "I'll admit that with them taste isn't paramount, but for a variety of textures and visual delight, they are ahead."

"But you can't discount taste in eating. I might put Indian food after Chinese and French, a really subtle curry or their slow-cooked chicken—but then how could I do that and overlook Greek food? Their spinach pies and lamb dishes, moussaka, stuffed grape leaves—"

"Have you tried really good Cuban cooking? Now there's full-bodied food. Or, for that matter, a good Spanish paella?"

"Good Lord, I've forgotten Italian! Can anything compare to a dish of spaghetti al pesto made with really fresh sweet basil and heavy cream?"

"Heavy cream in pesto sauce?"

"Oh, yes. You cut the oil in half and substitute cream. There's a little place downtown, one of those checked-tablecloth-and-candlelight places, that makes it that way, in season. It's incredible, and their zuppa di pesce . . ."

I feel a glow of pleasure just discussing it. "And fish restaurants. My God, what can compare to a real American shore dinner with steamed clams and lobsters and boiled corn?"

"Why, a thick cut of prime steak done very rare, the American way. Now that's pleasure."

"Don't forget the diners!" I remind him. "A good American diner with a loud heart-of-gold waitress and a skillful short-order chef! You can't beat that service or food, seriously."

José looks at his watch happily. "You know, it's almost time to eat."

Going, Going—Gone!

"I cannot resist an auction," Mimi confesses. "There is something about them that gets me. I suppose a good part of it is the treasure-hunting syndrome."

"What's that?"

"Well, you know, the idea that all of a sudden I'm going to come on a fabulous bargain that no one else is aware of, and I'll be able to buy it for a song."

"Has it ever happened?"

"Oh, yes. I was at a little country auction last year, and toward the end most of the people drifted off. There were just a few diehards like myself left, and the auctioneer was offering box after box of junk for next to nothing, just clearing them out. One box had a cast-iron toy on top that looked interesting, so I bid and got the whole box for five dollars.

"Mostly it was junk, old irons and toasters, but besides the toy I'd seen there were two very old cast-iron mechanical banks. One was an Uncle Sam bank and the other an elephant. I cleaned them up, and do you know, I saw those same banks in a reputable antique dealer's shop for two hundred dollars each! Now, that was a treasure."

"Is that the main pleasure you get out of auctions?"

"Oh, no. I think it's always there in the back of your mind, but my real pleasure is a gambler's pleasure. Bidding is a form of gambling. How high should I go? When should I stop? If I stop now won't the next bidder get it at a dollar more? Isn't it worth taking a chance and going a little higher?

"It's an exciting game, especially if you have a good auction-eer. He builds up a kind of charged excitement, and then something comes up that you know is valuable, and you think, Will anyone else recognize it? Can I get it at a good price? And you don't want to pass it up. Of course, ninety-nine times out of a hundred, someone else recognizes it too and bids you right up.

"You have to set a limit, and stay within that limit even if it breaks your heart. You have to know just what a thing is worth and stop at that point, otherwise you get out of control.

"But even when you don't get a bargain, or if you don't buy at all, there's a sparkling kind of excitement to the whole thing."

"What are your favorite auctions?"

"The country auctions, if they're authentic. I've been to auctions at the big galleries, but there's no real thrill there. Everyone has looked the stuff over and knows exactly what it's worth, and you're up against the pros.

"Oh, you can get a bargain in a sense, just because they are pros. Say you see a fine piece of furniture. You know that if a dealer buys it, he's going to mark it up for sale in his shop by 20 to 40 percent. If you bid against him and go, say 10 percent higher than he knows it's worth to him, he'll usually let it go and you've got something that would sell for 10 to 30 percent more than you paid. That's a bargain, but to do that you have to really know value and what things sell for—and of course you have to really, really want the thing because in any case you're taking a chance. The other bidder may not be a dealer, but another sucker like you!

"In a genuine country auction you can often get a sensational buy, just because there are fewer pros around. I've been to some where I'm sure there were no dealers.

"Of course, you still have to look out for the auctioneer's

helpers, who'll bid something up just to keep it from going at a bargain. It's illegal, but it's done. If you get an honest auctioneer, he just won't let the bidding start too low.

"Another pleasure I get out of auctions is watching the people around me. In the city auctions at the big galleries, there is always a sprinkling of famous types, and everyone buzzes with gossip. Did you see her? Do you know who she is? Do you know who he represents? And all that. And there are the very sleek ladies and the elegant men—oh, that's all fun!

"But in country auctions the bidders are usually local characters, like housewives bidding on kitchen equipment or men looking for instruments or tools. At one last summer there were about five hippie types from a local commune buying the strangest assortment of broken appliances and furniture. I lost track of the auction entirely just concentrating on them and wondering about their life-style.

"And then, of course, there's the handyman's special. There are always a few. I'm letting this go for a song because it has a slight damage. What am I bid? And of course the damage is that it won't work, but you don't really care.

"And I've come home with some mad white elephants. A press for juicing apples—you can make a quart of cider out of five dollars' worth of apples. And a carved mahogany sideboard that won't fit through my door, and a beautiful Oriental rug with a damaged center—oh, well, in a little while I can hold an auction of my own in my garage. Would you like to come?"

Pleasure in the Buff

"The Mad Mower has struck again," Lila tells me as we walk across her neatly cut lawn to the terrace.

"What do you mean, the Mad Mower?"

"That's what we call Bert when he mows the lawn. He always does it when no one's around."

"Why?"

"Because for some obscure reason he does it in the nude. I think it's absolutely insane, but he says he loves it."

Bert brings drinks out to the terrace. He's tall and lean and bronzed, the picture of health.

"I do love it," he says. "I suppose I'm a real nudity freak. I get so much pleasure out of doing anything in the raw—alone. I haven't yet reached the state where I can socialize without clothes. I haven't joined any nudist groups."

"Why not?"

He sips his drink and frowns. "I guess a group seems a little too organized. A great deal of the pleasure I get out of being nude is the spontaneity of the whole thing. It started one real hot day when I had to mow the lawn and there was no one else around. I stripped to my shorts and halfway through the job I said, What the hell, why keep my shorts on? The only one around is Lila, and I can't shock her, so I stripped all the way down."

"I was shocked," Lila laughs. "Not in the conventional sense, but it seemed so, well, incongruous to see a man mowing a lawn in the nude—though, to tell you the truth, a pair of shorts doesn't make that much difference."

"There's also the privacy factor," Bert says, coming back to my question. "I find something very private about nudity, and perhaps that's why I'm reluctant to get into any group activity. Last year we were looking for a vacation, and we saw a very inexpensive package deal called V.I.B. tours. I sent away for their literature, and found out that V.I.B. stood for vacations in the buff! We didn't go, partly because Lila just isn't into nudity and partly because I wasn't ready to make it a group deal."

"Because of your feelings about privacy?"

"Well, I've nothing against it theoretically, but my pleasure in it is purely sensual. I think that seeing other people nude would take away from my own involvement—although I understand that in situations like that you forget that you're nude very quickly.

"When I'm by myself, I tend to forget it. Initially, the pleasure is one of freedom. I don't feel bound up, swaddled, tied in—all the things that clothing does to me. I hate restricting clothes, jackets and ties, even though I have to put up with them in business. I always get into slacks and a T-shirt when I get home from work.

"But the step beyond that, out of my clothes altogether, is a giant step toward freedom. All right, I'll grant that mowing the lawn in the buff is a joke, but we have three acres of woods around our house here, and when I'm sure no one is on the grounds I'll take a walk through the woods in the nude. I get a wonderful physical sensation out of the touch of sun on my body, the wind and the cool air under the trees, the leaves brushing against me—I feel close to nature, a part of it. Maybe I'm just a throwback to the primeval man.

"But, you know, the feeling is also psychological. I feel at peace, close to nature in my mind as well as my body. And it doesn't have to be sunny and warm. I've gone walking without clothes in the rain, and that's a fantastic feeling.

"Boots and umbrellas and raincoats are designed to keep our clothes dry, but without clothes, who needs all that paraphernalia? There's no experience like feeling the rain fall on your bare skin, or, afterward, the sunlight drying your body.

"Once, when we were up here in the winter, I took a snow swim in the raw."

"What's a snow swim?"

"I just flung myself into a snowbank and rolled around in it. I couldn't do it for long, and I came tearing back into the house afterward, but while it lasted it was glorious!"

I look at Lila and ask, "Don't you ever feel you want to share it with Bert?"

She shrugs and looks down at her rather ample body. "I'm vain enough to want the dignity and concealment of clothes. Nudity is great for very young people, or people our age who are built like Bert. When we were first married we went upstate on our honeymoon and rented an island on a big lake, a whole island with a campsite all to ourselves.

"We put up a tent and ran around naked for two weeks. It was heavenly," she sighs. "But we were young, and I was proud of the way I looked. I enjoyed all the things Bert's told you about, the sun on my body, the rain, swimming naked in the lake—it was sensual, and sexual too. We were just married, you know, and discovering each other. But now"—she shakes her head—"I'll leave nudity to the Mad Mower."

Bert laughs. "You know, it's not only the out-of-doors that turns me on in terms of nudity. When I'm in the house alone, I often walk around without clothes. Again, there's a lack of restraint or restriction. And there's a mental feedback. Your mind begins to feel more open, more relaxed—maybe even more wholesome."

He nods. "I have a private theory that if we all did away with clothes, we'd do away with a lot of the idiocies of our civilization. It would open us up to a healthier view of sex and morality."

"Then why not join a nudist colony?"

"Well, maybe I will soon. I'm almost ready for it—if I can find one with a lawn that needs mowing."

The Eyes Have It

"Have you ever experienced the fantastic pleasure of communicating with your eyes alone?" Dana asks me at a cocktail party.

This is my field, body language, so I perk up at once. "Tell me what you mean?"

"Well," she looks around to make sure we aren't overheard. "Just before you came over I was flirting with that tall young man over there, the one with the blue eyes and black hair."

I see the man she indicates and I ask her, "From across the room?"

"Exactly. We didn't move toward each other at all. He's with a group I don't know. I think he came with the blonde with the big boobs, but, do you know, he's going to leave with me."

"How do you know?"

"Because we both spelled it out," she says, "and we did it all with eye contact. I caught his eye and looked away, and then looked back and caught him looking at me. Then he lowered his eyes to his drink, but I kept looking, and finally he looked up again and we stared at each other for a while, you know, just a little too long for it to be innocent.

"Oh, it was all so elaborate. He was talking to his friends all the while and they weren't aware of our signals, and I was talking to that awful shrink over there and he didn't know what was going on—and there we were, two total strangers across a crowded room saying with our eyes, Hello, I think you're the most interesting person in the room. Do you like me? Yes, oh, yes! Can we get to know each other better? Why sure. Let's blow this joint with each other."

"Now, wait," I interrupt. "I can get all the other signals, but let's leave with each other? How did you do that?"

She grins and widens her very lovely dark eyes. "All I did was this." She casts a sideways glance at the room where we all put our coats, then at the clock and then the door. "A one-two-three progression, and it worked."

"Of course. I can see that."

"So could he. He nodded and looked at the clock, then at his friends, at the blonde and at the cloakroom. Now as soon as it's decently possible I'll excuse myself to our hostess, get my coat, and go to the door. I'm willing to bet two to one that he'll be there with me."

"Your odds aren't good enough, but I'll watch."

She was right, of course. She spoke to the hostess as her "pick-up" made some excuse to his friends, and they were both, by some strange coincidence, at the door together.

It shouldn't have surprised me, because the eyes are indeed the most expressive part of our body, and I've played dozens of games with eye contact and had some very pleasant moments —and some very awkward ones.

Psychologists tell us there is a moral looking time, the length of time we can hold someone else's gaze without causing discomfort. It varies with circumstances. It's almost nonexistent in an elevator; there you don't dare look someone else in the eye for any length of time. It's a little longer in a bus, and even longer on the street.

I've walked along the avenue playing the eye game. I'll catch someone's eye—we all do, and the "proper" thing is to look away and by so doing signal, *I have no interest in you.* But sometimes, just for the fun of it, I will hold the gaze for a bit longer than the socially acceptable time. How long is the acceptable time? Well, we all know it because we're raised with eye contact as a part of our culture, just as we know what a wink or a smile means. But when I hold someone else's glance a bit too long I get a number of reactions.

Some people look away slightly annoyed. Others look back with interest. *Do I know you? Would you like to meet me?*

I've tried it with women older than I am, and occasionally I get an annoyed look or an unfriendly scowl. Ah, but sometimes I get a delightful reaction. The woman knows the game and recognizes the signal. *I am interested in you.* And, although she has no intention of continuing the flirtation, her head goes up with a touch of pride and her walk is a bit happier, and you can almost hear her think, Someone thought me attractive enough to give me the eye!

With a younger woman, the reaction is usually a faint offense. At your age!

With men, it's mixed. Some men will break stride and you'll see the question in their eyes, *Do I know him?* Rather than offend, they'll often smile and nod. Some stop and say, "Hello. How are you?"

I did it once to a smartly dressed Hollywood type coming out of a lavish New York hotel. He didn't break stride, but put out his hand quickly—good reflexes—and said, "Haven't seen you in a long time."

It was true. I said, "How are things with you?" adding, "out there." It was a safe bet he was from out of town. We had a five-minute conversation in which he rather desperately tried to find out who I was and where we had met. When we left I had the same kind of inner pleasure a child feels when he's gotten away with something particularly naughty. All from a glance held a fraction too long!

Foraging

Enid has cooked dinner for the four of us. There's a beautiful bass that Alvin caught in the lake this afternoon, broiled to perfection, but the rest of the meal looks completely unfamiliar.

Enid serves and asks brightly, "Can I give you some milkweed florets?"

Surprised, I ask, "What? Did you say milkweed?"

Alvin laughs. "Didn't Enid tell you, or is it supposed to be a surprise? Tonight's dinner was completely foraged. It all comes from the land."

Enid nods. "I did want to surprise you. I get so much pleasure out of gathering wild foods that most people ignore. I either make an entire meal out of them or stretch out my regular menu. Take these milkweed florets. They're the cooked green buds, just before the flowers open. Taste some."

I put a helping on my plate and taste it suspiciously. To my amazement it's delicious, a cross, it seems, between asparagus and broccoli, and yet not quite like either. "And this is a weed."

"You can't just cook it. You have to pour boiling water over it and cook it three times to get rid of the bitter principle, but it's worth it. And this is poke. That's a weed too. Later in the summer the whole plant is poisonous, but in spring the tender little sprouts make a wonderful vegetable."

I taste the poke, again an elusive but delicious flavor, not quite like anything I've had before. There's a salad of fresh dandelion greens and very young chicory and a dish of wild mushrooms to go with the fish. At first I balk at the wild mushrooms. "How do you know they're not poisonous?"

Enid shakes her head. "That's the first question everyone asks. Of course, there are poisonous mushrooms growing wild and I wouldn't touch them—or any edible species that resembles them even faintly. I collect the wild ones that can't possibly be poisonous.

"These are beefsteak mushrooms. They're hard to find, but delicious if you prepare them right. You have to slice them first and soak them in salt water, but you can't mistake them for anything else. They grow on logs and stumps and they're like brackets or fans and red on top with yellow undersides. They're the closest thing to meat in the vegetable world. Try some."

I take a taste uneasily. "I could eat them, but they bother me." Still, a second spoonful tastes better. It's obviously a taste that grows on you. "Do you cook like this often?" I ask Enid.

"Yes, but most wild plants are seasonal. You can only find these in the spring. I get a lot of pleasure out of foraging. Part of it is identifying the plant, knowing that in a small way I'm living off the land."

"And I get pleasure out of seeing our vegetable bills go down," Alvin says. "Enid finds an amazing number of things on her walks."

"The side of the road is best," Enid tells me. "Wild blackberries grow like weeds in August and you can get loads of them, and raspberries too. They're rarer but even more delicious. The pokeweed is best in the early spring and so are the milkweed florets. The daylilies you can pick right into August."

"Daylilies? The flowers?"

"No, the buds. You can't hurt the plant by gathering them—they're plentiful, and picking a few will force the plant to put out more. You get them when they're orange, just before they open, and you can fry them plain, or dip them in batter first, braise them, or even dry them out and use them all year round.

"Everyone knows about dandelion greens, but that chicory in the salad—that's another spring vegetable. You have to get it when it's very young. You know chicory? Those lovely blue flowers that bloom along the road in the summer?

"And if you're really adventurous—well, in wild mushrooms alone there are so many edible kinds. Some are sensational! There are all kinds of things growing that no one realizes are good to eat, like cattails. When they're very young you can cook and eat them like corn, and you can cook the roots, too. The early shoots of knotweed are a fine vegetable, and if you like strong tastes there are wild mustard and watercress and pigweed—my goodness, so many weeds that can be cooked as vegetables."

Bewildered by her list, I go back to the cooked milkweed and poke and Alvin's bass. We eat awhile, and then Enid says, "There's fun in cooking wild weeds as well as in collecting them. I consider it a challenge to make them as appetizing as commercial vegetables, but there's also the pleasure of simply knowing they're foraged stuff."

"And, you know," Alvin adds, "it's not just a country pleasure. While visiting New York City last spring we took a walk in Central Park and found just about every edible weed, including a luscious stand of knotweed, the shoots all pushing through the ground begging to be harvested. We were staying at a hotel, otherwise I'd have been tempted to pick a bundle."

We finish the meal with Colombian coffee and Enid apologizes. "There are so many natural drinks I could have served, but Al loves his coffee. You know, chicory root, if it's roasted and ground, makes a good coffee substitute."

"Strong as hell," Alvin tells me, "but the French add it to coffee, and it gives it a little something extra."

"And there are all sorts of teas you can make from dried wild plants, like mullein leaves—the kids call them elephant ears—and clover blossoms with peppermint leaves, even blackberry and raspberry leaves, if they're well dried. And sassafras root makes a drink like root beer." Her eyes sparkle as she lists the different plants.

I sip my coffee and wish she had served one of her teas. Tomorrow, I decide, I'll have to take a walk with Enid to see just what pleasure there is in gathering weeds.

A View from the Train

Darryl and I come back from a ride on the narrow-gauge railway that runs into Colorado's San Juan Mountains from Durango.

"You know," he says, "I'm a train nut. Not the kind that's turned on by an old-fashioned steam engine or a narrow-gauge railway—the old steam engine wasn't all that comfortable. Today's ride was fun, but a tough one. What I really like about train travel is watching the scenery. I take trains constantly."

I'm a little surprised at that. "In this age of airplanes?"

Darryl shrugs. "I don't travel by train to get anywhere fast. I travel for pleasure. I take all my vacations by train."

"But why, when train travel is decaying so?"

"Because I get a wonderful feeling for the different parts of the country. To me, train travel is a constant reminder of history. You know, heading west from Omaha, the trains travel the route the Mormons took years ago—through Denver, north to Cheyenne, and on to Utah. They walked all the way, and I get a tremendous kick out of looking at the land go by and comparing the hours it takes by train with the months it took them on foot.

"Crossing Nevada by train, going through that God-forsaken desert, you keep wondering what ever drove people to go west. Sometimes I think Brigham Young stopped where he did because his scouts said there just wasn't anything farther west.

"And then there's the train out of Reno across the Sierra Nevada range." His eyes glow as he remembers. "It starts climbing almost within the city limits, alongside the Truckee River, and it goes up into the mountains along the same route the Donner party took. I rode that train in May and there were still four feet of snow—more than I've ever seen back East! I got so much pleasure out of watching that route unfold from the security of my railroad coach."

"But still," I protest, "the trains today are in such bad condition."

"Yes, the engines are often new, but you're right: the cars usually date back to the fifties, before the railways tried to eliminate passenger service. But that touch of nostalgia that I get from the old coaches is fun to me. I can hear the echoes of political speeches to small-town audiences from the back cars of trains. We were such a cocky country then, so sure we would prosper indefinitely. And it's still so beautiful.

"When I head back East I usually take the northern route, sometimes only twenty-five miles south of the Canadian border, from Seattle along the Columbia River. I think of Lewis and Clark and realize how the river was when they traveled down it. Now I see the tremendous dams and locks—but the country is still open, so enormous and so empty.

"You can sit in your cities and read the newspapers about the rest of the country, or fly over it in an airplane, and it never seems real. When you see the land itself as the train crosses it, then you really know what it looks like. You realize the size and complexity of it, and you understand why people in, say, Kansas would have different attitudes and expectations from people living in New York or California."

He shakes his head. "It's a beautiful country, but it could so easily be ruined. You realize how right the conservationists are."

"Do you get any pleasure out of meeting different people on the train?"

Darryl shrugs. "Oh, I meet a few nice people, sure, but that's not my biggest pleasure. In fact, I try to avoid the chatty types in the observation cars. I'm not traveling to meet people, but to look and think." He spreads his hands. "I'm stimulated by thinking, as I go through the country, So that's how the world lives, by catching little vignettes of life along the way."

"Do you think we should bring back the railroads as they were?"

He shrugs. "How could we? They're just not efficient for long trips. Who could take three days and nights to go to California from New York when you can get there in hours by plane? Look, when you come right down to it, I'm not wild about life on the train. The only fun in eating on a train is that it gives you something to do. The food is never good.

"But you can't beat a train for giving you the historical sense of the country—and how it relates to today. I guess it's very much an intellectual pleasure. For instance, I used to see the whole countryside littered with abandoned cars, but now there are very few. Why? Well, I've figured out that today's high price of metal makes it profitable to haul the cars away. Obvious, perhaps, but I get a kick out of figuring out little details like that.

"When I go through cities by train I can see the decay of the downtown areas and the growth of shopping malls in the outskirts, and it's as though I'm feeling the pulsebeat of the country."

"Are all today's trains going downhill?"

"No, there are still some good ones. The best is the *Zephyr* from Chicago to Denver, then Cheyenne, Reno, over the mountains to Sacramento and San Francisco—that's the best long ride. But the trip south from San Francisco to Los Angeles is a great one—really beautiful, especially along the coast when you see the beaches and the ocean.

"And there's the *Superchief* from Los Angeles to Chicago on the Santa Fe route. It's dry country, but so scenic. And north from San Francisco to Seattle, you see the beautiful northwestern mountains—then you can take the *Empire Builder* through the state of Washington and the Idaho border—those trains are all good."

"What about the trains east of the Mississippi?"

"They used to be great, but not now. I hear the train down the coast to Florida isn't bad, but I haven't ridden it lately. The trip from New York to Chicago is a disaster, always late. And those Penn Central tracks!

"The sad thing is we're forgetting trains. I've seen rusting tracks in upstate New York where the scenery is breathtaking. Because of economy, comfort, expediency—for one reason or another they go out. Of course, you can't turn time back, but if you ride the trains that are left you can, in a way, see back in time—and that's where I get my pleasure!"

No Place to Go but Up

Steve and I rest on a small ledge in the San Juan Mountains of Colorado, and he points up to a sheer pink cliff towering above a sloping forest of conifers. "Now that would be a great climb."

I shiver, still breathless from our long walk up the trail from the lodge. "You'd have to be a human fly!"

"No way! That's not a hard climb. I'd really enjoy it—if I had the equipment."

I look at him in mild astonishment. "Enjoy it? What pleasure could you get out of that?"

He considers my question seriously. "Well, let's see. First there's the enjoyment of moving over a beautiful terrain, looking down from the heights at the land—the scenic, visual pleasure. But I guess the real heart of it all is making the ascent so that it's absolutely safe."

I stare at the cliff. "Safe?"

"A lot of the fun is having people like you, who don't know the ins and outs of rock-climbing, react like that. Sure, it looks risky."

"How did you get into rock-climbing?"

Steve shrugs. "I guess it's part of the basic urge to climb that every kid gets—you know, when you're young it sends you right up the apple tree in the back yard. When you're too old for trees you look for something else you can climb. Climbing's a very muscular sport, but the real secret is in balance, using as little energy as you can to keep yourself on the rock. If you really learn to climb well, you're able to look at a cliff with an educated eye and see the natural lines, the breaks and faults and slopes that allow you to walk up almost as if it were a ladder."

I squint at the rock face. "Some ladder! And you get pleasure out of that?"

"Actually, the pleasure is a combination of intellectual and physical effort in surroundings of great beauty. It's a tactile pleasure too. Every rock has its own feel, and climbing is almost like a love affair with the rock. Your hands move over it as you go up, fitting to it, adapting to it."

"How is it intellectual?"

"Well, you're doing something that could be dangerous, but doing it safely, protecting your strength and knowing when to back away from a climb that won't work—that's an intellectual approach."

"Do you climb alone?"

"Sometimes. There's a great deal of joy in solo climbing. When you accomplish something, you know you've done it yourself, depending on no one else. But there's a big element of risk involved. I enjoy it, but I don't approve of it. A good climbing team of two can take turns protecting each other." He locks his hands together, twining the fingers. "It builds a mutuality of purpose and trust, a very deep kind of friendship where you depend on someone else for your life.

"I had a partner for many years, and we were different in every way—our life-styles, our physiques—but we got along. It was a good arrangement. I don't think I've ever known a deeper pleasure than when the two of us were doing a free six."

"A free six? What's that?"

"Well, we grade climbs. Three is a walk-up, no rope; four you should use a rope, and five you must. There's a five-one, five-two, five-three . . . each harder. A free six is climbing with artificial aids, a hanging ladder of cables and tubes, pitons—metal spikes that you hammer into the rock face to support your rope."

I look at the looming pink cliff apprehensively.

"That's the most fun for me," Steve says. "Of course, doing without aids on a free six that demands them is even more fun. That's a real challenge!"

"How much of the pleasure is in the challenge?"

He considers that for a moment. "That's hard to say. It's a great feeling to look at a cliff and realize you're capable of scaling it. Sure, there's a great deal of personal challenge, yet . . ." He hesitates. "Myself, I'll take any reasonable challenge, but basically I'm a very gentle person. I honestly don't think I'm trying to prove anything." He's silent for another long moment, then with some honesty adds, "Except myself. I guess I'm constantly testing myself, and I enjoy passing the test.

"Most people have a fear of heights, but I enjoy that fear. I love to sit on a high mountain pinnacle, but the fear is still there, and in periods of stress it's very strong—but it's controlled.

"Like maybe I'm out on a face and I've overextended myself. Can I make the next spot, or must I retreat? I face the danger of using my strength up too quickly, which almost guarantees a fall.

"To me, the ultimate pleasure is to be in a spot like that, almost out of control, and then to consciously take my fear, bundle it into a ball, and tuck it away, and get back into control and do what I must. It's a kind of testing, and it generates a wonderful, quiet confidence in myself."

"You're telling me that the greatest pleasure comes at the moment of greatest danger?"

"Or right after it. If there were no danger there'd be no pleasure."

"Why?"

"Because control of that danger gives me the most pleasure. I'd put that above the joy of physical exertion and the visual pleasure of climbing. Let me tell you of the greatest single moment of pleasure I've experienced in climbing.

"It was on a cliff in New York State called Yellow Face, a marvelous rock—granite and conglomerate, very strong and stable, rough enough to get a good grip, with overhangs and cracks, horizontals and verticals. I went up with my partner, a free-six climb. The crux of it was a small slope of ten to fifteen feet with no holds, 150 feet above the ground.

"There was a good ledge to start from, and we moved horizontally away from that position on small holds with good piton protection. Then we tried to move up, starting from the top of an overhang. About ten feet up it got extremely difficult. I was into it, but I couldn't make it go. I felt that if I could move my feet and shift my weight I'd have it.

"It was chancy, but I went up into it, straining everything—and I fell.

"I was twelve feet above my piton, and I just went off, hanging free. My piton caught me beautifully because we'd rigged it so well, and I knew it would. Now that fall was frightening to me, but it was a pleasure as well! I scaled back to the ledge, rested, and then went up and did it again—successfully.

"That climb was safe, yet it appeared to be incredibly risky. You see, I knew that I could go up using every bit of my ability, that I might not make it, but that if I did fall it would be a controlled ride—that was my core of pleasure."

We both look up at the pink cliff now, and Steve nods. "I'd like to try this one. Shall I take you up and show you how it's done?"

"I don't think so!"

He laughs. "I wouldn't really take you unless you'd gone to a good rock-climbing school. That's the key to the pleasure of rock climbing—get the proper training first, experience the controlled danger next."

City Canyons, Country Lanes

Jenny says, "Come and take a walk. It's a beautiful day outside."

"Why is it," I ask, "that no one is happy to sit indoors and relax on a beautiful day? Isn't that just as pleasant as walking?"

"Not a bit!" Jenny grabs my hand. "Come on and I'll show you some of the pleasures of walking. Let's go downtown on the avenue, where we can window shop. That's half the fun of walking in a city. You know, I think window-dressing should be considered an art form. The big department stores do beautiful jobs. Look what this store does with shoes!"

The store, an expensive one, has a window devoted to spring styles, but the shoes are all displayed as the ears of papier-mâché Easter bunnies. Another window shows raincoats in a swirling shower of plastic streamers of mock rain. In another, chiffon skirts are blown by hidden fans.

"And Christmas!" Jenny says. "That's a wonderful time for

walking. Every store tries to outdo its neighbor. There's something to see on every block. One store has a chimney with a puppet Santa coming out every quarter hour. Another has the whole window divided into rooms like a giant doll house with antique figures recreating an old fashioned Christmas.

"But even on nonholidays like today, there's so much to see—jewelry store windows with antique rings, bookstores with all the bright covers and posters. Look at that head shop with the astrological charts and the candles! Who'd dare burn them? And that dress shop, the little boutique— Come on, let's cross and look in the window."

Letting Jenny lead the way, I try to get into the swing of things—and soon I'm doing the leading. "Come over here and look at this antiques shop," I tell her. "Isn't that a great collection of toy banks?" And Jenny smiles knowingly.

When I tell my friend Mark how much fun I had with Jenny on our walk, he nods and says, "I'm not a window-shopper, but I'm very much into walking, too. You see, I'm an architecture freak. I walk through the city constantly, never take buses and taxis. I get the biggest charge out of identifying buildings."

"How do you mean?"

"I mean historically. I love those classic Victorian brownstones, and I get such fun out of suddenly discovering one I've never seen before, though I may have passed it a dozen times. Then there are the apartment houses and office buildings done in Art Deco style, with those crazy 1920 designs, the stylized birds and geometric patterns. Sometimes I'll find a building put up before the turn of the century, maybe pseudo Gothic, or even Art Nouveau—they're great.

"Then, of course, there are the modern glass and metal dinosaurs. You walk down a street of them and it's a real trip into the future. But, even more amazing, sometimes I'll find a wooden house of two or three stories squeezed between two big brick apartment houses—that makes the little house look like a real relic, even though it might not be all that old.

"Another thing that turns me on when I walk," Mark adds, "is the statuary on buildings. There are stone carvings all over, but we hardly ever notice them. All you have to do is raise your eyes at just about any building put up before the thirties—and even some during the thirties—and you'll see all sorts of carvings. Animals and human, heads above the doorways or whole figures. One hotel downtown has a fabulous relief of a male and female nude lying on their sides over the entrance, like two Michelangelo figures on a tomb. You can't see them because of the hotel's awning, but if you stand across the street it's just great—corny, but great.

"And there's a fountain in the park with carved sandstone panels that are terrific. Every one is different. When I walk I keep looking through the city for new pieces of carving, tops of windows in old tenements, details on skyscrapers—no one appreciates the work in that sculpture. That's what makes walking through the city so great."

Another friend, Estella, can't be bothered with architecture. "When I walk, I just can't look up that high. I'm a people-watcher. I love to walk along the street and see the variety of different people, so many different types of faces. I wish I were an artist or a good photographer. I'd capture all of them. You know, this country is such a melting pot, the cities especially.

"But here in the city there are also such varieties of behavior. Some get pretty nutty! Yesterday I saw a man walking along arguing furiously with no one at all. And the crazy ladies—the ones who live out of shopping bags and baby carriages filled with their junk! Plus the garbage scavengers, men and women who stop at every garbage can and sift through it. Some of them aren't a bit ashamed, and some are even well dressed—browsing for God knows what.

"Then there's a phone-booth nut I always see in midtown. He scrounges through all the phone-booth return slots looking for returned coins. He's so systematic and methodical about it, I wonder if he keeps books and pays an income tax on what he gets!

"And hustlers! Everyone seems to be selling something. I once saw an old Chinese man selling pictures embroidered in silk, exquisite work, for next to nothing. And there's a shabby, wild fellow, enormously fat, who sells brass belt buckles for two and three dollars. He has a real hustler approach, shouting at the crowds even before he sets up his display case.

"Oh, I could walk through the city every day and never get bored—as long as there are people."

I shake my head. "I enjoyed my walk with Jenny, and, sure, people are fun, but when I walk I really like the country. I like to walk alone, to find a new patch of woods, a stream or a little pond, a stand of white birch or a bed of wildflowers. I remember coming out of the woods once into a little meadow that slanted up to the hills beyond, and the entire meadow was carpeted with golden-rod. It was like a sheet of gold, so lovely that I just stood there staring for I don't know how long. Things like that give me pleasure, especially when I discover them alone."

Estella says, "Oh, but where's the sense of discovery without other people?"

"That's just it. When I walk I like to explore nature. People obliterate it and spoil it. When I'm alone I can drink it in, absorb it, really see it—that's how I get my pleasure."

The Heat's on

My vacation had been long delayed, and when I finally got away to the summer lodge, I inevitably overdid it. By late afternoon of the first day I could hardly move. I made it to the side of the pool, but I felt too stiff to get into the water.

"As bad as all that?" my friend Oscar asked sympathetically.

"A little worse, but it's my own fault. I was as greedy as a kid with a charge account in a candy shop."

"Well, let's get a little steam and soften you up."

I looked apprehensive. "Should I? I've never been in a steam room."

"You're kidding! Why, that's the best medicine for stiff muscles. Come on."

We went through the men's locker room, discarded our suits, picked up towels, and entered the steam room behind the showers. The lodge was built of redwood and rock, and the steam room was rock-walled with tile floors and benches. My first impression was of overwhelming heat, clouds of it. I sat down on a tiled bench, flinching at the heat, and leaned back gingerly, to find to my surprise that the heat was bearable. In fact, soon it was very pleasant.

I drew in a tentative breath and closed my eyes. I had never been warm in this way, warm in every part of my body. There was a sensation of floating in warmth, being cradled in warmth, pulling it into my lungs, and feeling it penetrate every pore.

After a few minutes I became aware that my assorted aches and pains were gradually easing, that the heat was penetrating beneath the surface of my skin and gently easing my cramped muscles. I stretched out full length with a grateful sigh and gave myself willingly to the steam's caress.

Since that time I've become something of a steam freak. My favorite setup is the steam room at the local gym. There I can work out until my muscles are pleasurably tight, loosen up with a few laps in a cool pool, and then sit back in the steam room and let the penetrating warmth sink into my body and loosen all my muscles.

That first day in the summer lodge my friend Oscar gave me some basic points about steam baths.

"First of all," he said, "don't overdo it. There's a tremendous temptation to stay in the steam room too long. It's so comfortable and restful. But fifteen minutes should be your outer limit. And you have to cool down afterward. You sweat a good deal in a steam room, and you keep sweating for half an hour after you come out. Get dressed too soon and you end up with a wet shirt.

"Make sure your steam room isn't too hot. That can weaken you terribly. There's a restful heat, between 160 and 180 degrees, that will steam out the aches without straining you. You know your body fights to keep you at a normal temperature, and if the steam is too hot, or if you take it too long, that fight exhausts you. Ride with the heat. That's the trick of enjoying it."

I've found that he was right. I ride with it, letting it flow over me and around me. I don't believe any of the claims some people make about steam flushing the wastes from your system or taking off weight. To me it's simply a pleasant, sensual experience. I'm wrapped in warmth, cradled and soothed, and my muscles are loosened up. I feel relaxed and pampered.

"If you like steam," another friend told me, "you ought to try the sauna. That's a dry heat. It's different—not better or worse, but different."

It didn't take much urging after my pleasant introduction to steam, and I found that he was right. There's no sense in comparing the two. They both deliver heat to the total body, and both are sensual experiences. There is more sweating in a sauna, and some people find this more pleasant. For others, it's a minus factor.

I've tried saunas in the mountains after cross-country skiing, and once in a little valley in Vermont where a Finnish friend had built a redwood sauna next to a cold mountain stream. We sweated for almost half an hour, and then, reluctantly on my part, enthusiastically on his, plunged into the cold water. I didn't enjoy it, but my friend was in ecstasy.

Afterward, over a glass of brandy, he explained, "It's the invigoration that pleasures me. I can feel my blood come alive, feel my whole body glow with health."

I shivered and shook my head. "I like the sauna. I find it warm and relaxing, but plunging into the cold water seems like some sort of Spartan testing. I forced myself to do it, but I didn't like it at all."

"The doctors say it's healthy."

"I wonder about that. I think the cold shock can be a strain on someone who's not used to it. With steam or sauna my pleasure is in comfort, in relaxation, in a luxurious easing of my muscles—a restful pleasure."

He shook his fine Finnish head. "Not for me. My pleasure is in the sharp contrast between hot and cold, in the waking up of my entire body, my muscles and nerves. I come alive, and that's pleasure!"

I shrugged, saying, "I guess one man's cold is another man's pleasure."

The Games We Used to Play

There were twelve of us at Al's summer place, teen-agers and adults, and we sat around on the patio in the late afternoon of an autumn day, all reluctant to admit how bored we were.

"When I was a kid," Al said abruptly, "we'd never let an afternoon like this go to waste."

Jon, fourteen years old, said, "What would you do?"

"We'd play Ringalevio. This is a perfect evening for it."

"What's Ringalevio?" another teen-ager asked, more out of politeness than respect.

"It's a great game," I said, thinking back with a thrill of pleasure. "We would divide ourselves up into two teams and we needed a big area, like an empty lot, with a boundary line down the middle."

Al points to the meadow behind his house. "You could use a spot like that. All you need is a divider."

"How about the fence?" Jon asks, nodding at the straggling fence that roughly divides the meadow in half.

"Of course!" All at once Al is excited, and his excitement begins to infect the rest of us. "First we choose sides, then toss for territories. Each territory has a jail, a spot about ten feet by ten, and you range up and down the border having pulling contests, tug-of-wars, trying to pull someone over to your side. Then you keep him on your territory while you yell 'Ringalevio one-two-three,' three times. Then he's a prisoner and goes to jail."

"That's right," I say. "And he stays there till someone from his team invades the territory and races through the jail yelling, 'Free all!' Then you all run back for your own territory."

"Unless you catch someone trying to free a prisoner and you hold him till you yell 'Ringalevio one-two-three,' three times."

"And of course, you can make daredevil raids into enemy territory just as a challenge, if you're fast enough to evade anyone who tries to catch you."

There's a sort of awed pause, and then Jon says, "Far out!" He jumps up. "Well, come on. What are we waiting for?"

I look at Al, and then at the rest of his guests, at least half of my own age. "It's kind of strenuous . . ."

"Sometimes I think all you want to do is talk about the good old days. Come on, let's try and relive them," one of the under-twenties challenges.

We can't resist. Sides are chosen, boundaries set, and in the early evening half of us try to rediscover our youth while the other half tries to understand what was once so much fun.

Amazingly, it works! Awkward at first, the game soon settles in as our true natures take over. Bob is a daredevil, always racing into enemy territory. Sarah hangs along the border, always looking for a challenge, confident of her power in a tug-of-war. Jon is captured and shouts for release, and the rest of us dart back and forth in the autumn twilight, breathless, shouting, letting ourselves plunge into the sheer pleasure of reckless physical activity.

The game ends with darkness and no conclusive winners. Half of us are completely exhausted, and the other, younger, half high with excitement.

"Hey, what were some other games you used to play?" Jon asks as we settle down in the living room with drinks.

We begin to dredge our memories. We had so much fun when we were young—but what did we do?

"Well, no one plays Botticelli any more," Al says suddenly. "Now that's a good sitting-down game."

"What's Botticelli?"

"A guessing game about famous people, like Twenty Questions. That's another good one."

Sarah asks, "Is that like Animal, Vegetable, Mineral?"

Something from many years back suddenly clicks, and I say, "I know a wonderful guessing game. You don't guess a person or an object, but an entire story."

"What?" "How?" "How long would it take?" The questions are eager.

"Clarence, you want to be a writer," I say to one of the under-twenties. "Let's start with you. Go out of the room where you can't hear us, and we'll think up the plot for a story. When you come back you ask us questions to which we can only answer yes or no. You have to uncover the plot by your questions, and we give you a time limit, let's say thirty minutes."

Annie, our hostess, says, "No more, because we're having dinner in an hour."

Clarence goes out of the room and I tell the others, "There is no plot. The first one to answer Clarence's question says yes, the next one no. We alternate around the room, yes, no, yes, no—get it? He constructs his own plot."

The game is a grand success, but regrettably it can only be played once with the same group. Clarence's plot is wild and devious, involving incest on an antebellum Southern plantation with a science-fiction time-travel switch—all out of his own fertile imagination. Al, a psychoanalyst, is delighted.

Later, after dinner, Jon confesses, "I haven't had this much fun in a long time. What other games did you used to play?"

"There's Murder, of course."

"How do you play that?"

"Not after Ringalevio!" Al protests. "Some other night. You

need a big house and—let's see. You draw slips from a hat and one person draws a slip saying murderer, another detective, and you know—butler, master, mistress, maid, mysterious visitor from the past. You make up your characters. Then you roam around the house till the murderer gets somebody alone, tells him he's the victim, arranges his death, then leaves clues. The detective has to solve it. It's elaborate, and fun for a rainy day."

"Or a rainy night," I add.

"On a rainy night," Sarah recalls, "we used to play Sardines."

Jill, a teen-ager, lifts her eyebrows. "That sounds intriguing."

"Well, let's see. We'd put out most of the lights and whoever was 'it' would hide in a small place, like a closet or under a bed. The rest of us would start looking and when one of us found 'it' we'd slip in with him—or her—and stay quiet. One by one everyone would find 'it' and end up under a bed, or packed in a closet like sardines. The last one left was 'it' for the next game."

"I like that!" Jill nods.

"As I remember, it was a youngsters' game."

"And there was charades," Annie says.

"We still play that at college."

"There were the old card games like Go Fish, and Concentration—and Finish the Tale."

"What was that?"

Annie smiles. "I loved that. We'd sit in a circle, and someone would start making up a story and tell it for exactly five minutes, and then the next person would pick it up for the next five minutes and so forth. The real fun was in the way each person twisted the plot around to suit their own interests. One boy could always be counted on for sex, and there was a girl who always introduced the psychological conflict. The toughest, I always thought, was the last five minutes, where it all had to be wound up neatly. The most fun was developing a real cliff hanger and passing it on to the next teller. You had to always be consistent and logical and make the characters act normally."

"Let's play that!" Jill begs.

"Can't we play Murder before bedtime?" Jon suggests.

"I'm for Sardines. Everyone doesn't have to play if they're not up to it."

We all laugh, and Al says, "There's another game called Post Office, and of course there's Spin the Bottle, and—"

"Hey! When did you find time to do anything else?" an under-twenty asks.

Thoughtfully, Al says, "There was a lot more time in those days—a lot more!"

The Gifts and the Giving

"Let me give you a cigar," Sean says. "This is really a tremendous blend, like the smoothest Havana."

"You really shouldn't," I protest. "Barbara and I invited you and Meg to dinner, and you've brought a bottle of wine, dessert, and now the cigars!"

"It's my pleasure," Sean insists, and watches me with a smile as I sample the cigar.

"That's really good!" I look at his happy face with its bushy eyebrows and shock of white hair. "It really does give you pleasure, giving people things."

He shrugs, slightly uncomfortable. "Now you're not going to get into the psychological bit, how I'm trying to buy love and affection—"

"No—it's only that so many people get pleasure out of receiving gifts—I think most of us do. But you seem to get more pleasure out of giving."

Sean smiles. "But all those people who get the gifts are given them by other people who must get pleasure out of giving."

I think a moment. "I guess you're right."

"I don't think I'm unusual," Sean says. "But when I can give someone else a gift that pleases them, I feel a deep peace within myself. The real pleasure of giving lies in pleasing, in knowing that someone else is enjoying something you selected—and I guess in sharing."

"How sharing?"

"Like that cigar. I know how good it is because I've smoked the brand. I discovered them, but my enjoyment is doubled if I get to share that discovery. To see you enjoy the cigar is truly a pleasure to me."

Barbara agrees with Sean. "I feel that way about books. When I read one I really like, I want to share it. I remember when we first discovered that delightful book of Jack Finney's, *Time and Again*. I went out and bought three copies for gifts, and I knew just the people I was going to give them to, people who'd enjoy that kind of story. And *Shogun*, that novel about Japan. It was such a good book I wanted to share it, so I bought an extra copy to give away. That sharing is a big part of the pleasure."

Sean's wife, Meg, looks up from her needlepoint. "You know, when the kids see a movie they love, they always want to share it with you. They drive you frantic by telling you every part of the plot, but really, in a sense, they're giving you something, the same as when you give a book you like to a friend."

"There is a pleasure in giving," Barbara says, "and I guess it's tied up with what you give. I was thinking of my daughter's birthday. I was going to give her money, but to me that seemed so cold and thoughtless, as if I hadn't taken the trouble to choose anything special. Instead I bought her a gift and my pleasure was in the selecting of it and then in her reaction to it—kind of a double pleasure."

Meg nods. "I like to make my own gifts. Needlepoint takes a lot of time, but I've made small pillows and glass cases and belts for my friends. That gives me a double pleasure, like Barbara said."

"Like my cigars," Sean says. "I didn't make them, but I found them, and I wanted you to share what I found."

"Like my paper wallets," Barbara adds. "I discovered some beautiful Japanese paper wallets and I bought one. Then because it was so lovely I kept going back and buying others for friends I knew would appreciate them. I get so much pleasure out of seeing other people's reactions to them."

"To really understand the pleasure of giving," Meg says as she puts down her needlework, "you have to remember those gifts our kids used to make us in school—the woolen picture frames, the homemade cards, the felt bookmarks. They gave them to us with such love, offering all the effort and time they had put in along with the gift. I'd always choke up when I got something like that because I could see their pleasure glowing in their faces."

"But the real test of pleasure in giving," Barbara says after a moment, "is the anonymous gift. My brother-in-law used to do that. He'd give something to a friend or relative without letting them know he was the giver. When I asked him why, he said, 'It takes the embarrassment out of giving, yet it leaves the fun in.' "

"I don't understand that," Meg frowns.

"Well, you'd have to know him. He couldn't bear to be thanked for doing a favor. He felt that what he got out of doing it was enough. Gratitude embarrassed him, and he felt that in some way it demeaned the person who got the gift."

"But so much of the pleasure of giving is in the reaction of whoever gets the gift," Meg protests. "And a great part of the pleasure of receiving a gift is seeing the giver's reaction to *your* reaction!"

Barbara nods. "That's true, but maybe the whole act of giving should be a little—purer. If you could separate that reaction from giving, would you still give? Wouldn't that eliminate the giving that is only a way of buying affection or approval?"

I stand up and bring in the wine, Sean's gift. "Let's not get into that. Let's open the wine and feel a little affection for the giver!"

Good Night—Sweet Dreams

"To Mary, Queen, all praise be given. She sent the blessed sleep from heaven, which slid into my soul," Jerry says. "That's what Coleridge said about sleep, and it's what I feel too. When I sleep through the night—fall asleep easily and don't wake up until morning—I feel as if I've been given a fantastic gift, the most pleasure I can get in my day-to-day life."

"Your age is showing," Marcia says. "When a man thinks of bed as only a place to get some blessed sleep, he's beginning to get too old."

"If you'll tell me how to stop the aging process . . ." Jerry laughs.

"Not that, but the aging in your mind," Marcia tells us. "Aging is physical, sure, but it's also psychological." She looks around at the group of us, all talking about the pleasures of sleep, and she says, "No matter how old your body is, your mind can still stay young."

"Depending on your circulation," Don adds. "But I'm still in my twenties, and I go along with Jerry. To me, nothing beats the pleasure of falling into a deep dreamless sleep, and waking up so refreshed you're like a new person."

Suziko says, "There's truth in that, but to me a large part of the pleasure of sleep is how you sleep. I like my bedroom peaceful, the colors muted and my bed low. I don't like the mattresses you Westerners use. I sleep on a futon on the floor with another on top of me."

"What's a futon?" Jerry asks.

"You might call it a Japanese comforter, but it's more than a comforter. They used to be stuffed with down, but now you find more polyester. They're so light they almost float on top of you—much lighter than blankets—and they insulate you perfectly in the coldest weather."

"Do you use them in summer too?"

"Well, if you need a covering, they're cooler than blankets, like—what's your word, gossamer? We also prepare ourselves for sleep. We never eat heavily before bed, and we don't think heavily."

"What do you mean, think heavily?"

"We think very soft thoughts. Consider something very beautiful, a vase of flowers, a view of the sea or the mountains, a tree, a rock even. We feel its inner structure and its peace, and allow that peace to flow into us."

We are all silent for a moment, then Marcia says, "I like to prepare myself for sleep with a scented bath, and then I'm very fussy about my sheets. I think the most wonderful breakthrough in sleep has been this whole new range of colored and designer sheets. They're a real trip! I love to have a matched set of flower-printed sheets with matching pillows, all color-coordinated to my room."

Diane says, "I like satin sheets. There's something so exquisitely luxurious and sensual about them—they add a whole new dimension to sleep."

Her husband, Ken, says, "Especially if you sleep in the nude. Satin against my skin turns me on. Maybe that's because it's generally frowned on for men to wear shiny fabrics like satin. I think of them as absolutely feminine, and to sleep between satin sheets, wow!"

"Well, it turns me on too," Diane says. "And I don't have your masculine-feminine problem. I think it's just the sensual touch of the material."

Don nods. "I agree, but for me furs are a turn-on too. I have this girl friend who keeps a couple of fur throws on her bed, and on cold nights she uses them with the fur side down and no sheets—it drives me up a wall!"

"How can you sleep, then?" Jerry asks.

"I can sleep, and beautifully. What I mean is that I become so aware of my sense of touch I swear I can feel every hair in the fur throw. One has short, silky fur and the other has rougher, longer hair. Each gives me a different sort of sensation—but they're both wonderful."

"Silks and satins and furs," Marcia says. "Oh yes, sleep should be luxurious, sensual, not only tactile but visual too, and olfactory. You should have screens and silk drapes and valances over your bed, plus incense. I visualize a sultan's tent for perfect sleeping pleasure!"

"And yet," I say thoughtfully, "the most wonderful night's sleep I ever had was out-of-doors. I was in my twenties, and my wife and I were on a hiking trip. We camped for the night near a mountain stream, and we slept on a ledge covered with moss near a small waterfall. I guess, though, we had all the stimuli you mentioned. The stars were brilliant and what we could see of the stream was beautiful, the moss under our sleeping bags was as soft as Don's furs and the waterfall was white noise to lull us. And as for incense, the smell of the green things around us, the mint and ferns, was better than any artificial scent. And, of course, there's always some extra pleasure in sharing a sleeping bag —especially when you're young."

We're quiet for a moment, and then my wife says, "I feel that all of these aids—sheets and furs and scents—are well and good, but at my age the greatest boon to sleep is my black mask."

"What's that?"

"A very, very comfortable satin mask lined with black silk. It blocks out the light. My husband can read as late as he wants, and thank heaven I can sleep! That's all I need for the blessed sleep from heaven to slide into my soul."

Index